Parish Finance

Parish Finance

Best Practices in Church Management

Michael J. Castrilli

Charles E. Zech

Foreword by Cardinal Donald Wuerl

Paulist Press
New York / Mahwah, NJ

Cover image (background): lmichman/bigstock.com
Cover & book design by Dawn Massa, Lightly Salted Graphics

Library of Congress Cataloging-in-Publication Data

Names: Castrilli, Michael J., author.
Title: Parish finance: best practices in church management / Michael J. Castrilli, Charles E. Zech; foreword by Donald Cardinal Wuerl.
Description: New York: Paulist Press, 2016. | Includes bibliographical references and index.
Identifiers: LCCN 2016018011 (print) | LCCN 2016028829 (ebook) | ISBN 9780809149957 (pbk. : alk. paper) | ISBN 9781587686221 (Ebook)
Subjects: LCSH: Catholic Church—Finance. | Church finance.
Classification: LCC BX1950 .C37 2016 (print) | LCC BX1950 (ebook) | DDC 254/.8—dc23
LC record available at https://lccn.loc.gov/2016018011

ISBN 978-0-8091-4995-7 (paperback)
ISBN 978-1-58768-622-1 (e-book)

Published by Paulist Press
997 Macarthur Boulevard
Mahwah, New Jersey 07430

www.paulistpress.com

Printed and bound in the
United States of America

Contents

Foreword

His Eminence
Cardinal Donald Wuerl
Archbishop of Washington

When I ask parishioners what they love about their parish, most will say the beauty of the liturgies or the number of outreach programs they have or the vitality of the parish school or their terrific pastor. It is not often that a parishioner will say, "Our financial management is excellent!" This is as it should be, for the vitality of the parish ought to be assessed by the quality of worship, community education, and service; but essential to the vitality of any parish is effective administration and sound stewardship.

As far back as the time of the early church, the Christian community understood the need for administration for harmonious communal life. In the Book of Acts, we learn that in the organization of the first community, attention was paid to the assessment of the resources of the community and their distribution among members and those most in need (Acts 2:42ff.).

It is no different today; the Church knows the importance of effective parish stewardship for the good of the overall mission. The Synod on the New Evangelization in 2012 affirmed that parishes, gathered in communion with their bishop and under the direction of the pastor, are called to be centers of the life of the Church. The bishops in the synod reaffirmed that the parish continues to be the primary presence of the Church in the neighborhoods, the place and instrument of Christian life that is able to offer opportunities to dialogue among people: for listening to and announcing the Word of God, for organic catechesis, for training in charity, and for prayer, adoration, and joyous Eucharistic celebration.

In our own Archdiocese of Washington Synod celebrated at our seventy-fifth anniversary, stewardship and administration were a significant focus alongside of all of the other areas of ministry that are at the heart of parish life. Among the synod recommendations that made their way into actual statutes were a number involving the call to provide parish leadership with financial and administrative guidelines, advice, and training to facilitate the regular pastoral planning that goes on in every parish.

How all of this ministry is carried out is where the responsibilities of the pastor and parishioners meet. In fact, The Decree on the Laity, from the Second Vatican Council, reflecting on the role of the laity in parish life, states, "Their activity within Church communities is so necessary that without it the apostolate of the Pastors is generally unable to achieve its full effectiveness" (Decree on the Apostolate of the Laity, 100).

In order to exercise this shared responsibility of pastor and parishioners, The Second Vatican Council recommended the establishment of two specific councils at the diocesan and parish level: a pastoral council and a finance council. The task of the parish pastoral council is to assist the pastor in his pastoral planning for the parish with expert opinion and advice for the good of the Church.

Recognizing the need for and importance of securing sound financial foundations, the Code of Canon Law, promulgated by St. John Paul II in 1983, mandates that every parish have a parish finance council. "Each parish is to have a finance council which is regulated by universal law as well as by norms issued by the diocesan bishop; in this council the Christian faithful" aid the pastor in the administration of the parish goods" (canon 537). While the two parish-level councils are separate and each has a different and specific role in the life and operation of the parish, they must work together for the good of the parish.

Michael Castrilli and Charles "Chuck" Zech do the Church a great service in *Parish Finance: Best Practices in Church Management*. Both authors are well versed in the pressing matter of good church management. For several decades, I have followed closely this commitment to help all of us in parishes respond effectively and responsibly to church management issues. In this book, they take us behind the scenes of an active parish to examine this collaborative relationship of the two councils and best practices in financial stewardship. Oftentimes, when we hear the word *stewardship* we think this is just about money. Michael Castrilli and Chuck Zech invite us to approach stewardship as the art of learning how to connect parish resources to achieve parish mission, vision, and goals" (pp. xiii–xiv). As befits any part of the life of a parish, this book teaches pastors and parish leaders how to work collaboratively toward increasing the vitality of the parish. The authors outline the relationship of prayer and discernment to pastoral planning, and pastoral planning to the development and execution of a budget. It is through discernment and assessment that the needs of parishioners become known, and through good budget execution that a parish is able to live within its means. Regardless of the size of the parish or the wealth of its parishioners, every parish has limited resources, and in the complex world in which we live today, ever-growing opportunities for ministry. This reality makes this book all the more important.

Our pastors come to parishes with varying degrees of knowledge of financial management. You can imagine how intimidating the details of administration and finances can be for a first-time pastor or even an experienced pastor moving from a small parish to a large parish that may include a school or a plant with multiple buildings. Many midsize and large parishes have budgets that equal those of small corporations. While pastors feel on firm ground preaching, teaching, and counseling, making decisions about everything from photocopier service contracts to investment portfolios can feel like walking on quicksand.

The contribution of *Parish Finance* is the clarity with which it guides a pastor and committee through a planning and budgeting cycle with an eye to good consultation, collaboration, and communication. Pastors and lay leaders will learn together how to make pastoral planning, budgeting, and financial transparency a regular part of parish life. Finance committees will learn that good stewardship is not focused on building big bank accounts and beautiful parish plants but rather on providing adequate resources for the parish to nurture and sustain the spiritual lives of its parishioners.

Here, we begin to appreciate the importance of a finance council and management team. On this team, the pastor finds a group of people ready to assist him in aligning financial resources to parish goals. The finance council allows the pastor to establish priorities, monitor the financial resources of the parish, and involve parishioners, who are the key stakeholders in the process.

A parish that institutes a pastoral planning process that enables it to discern how the Lord is calling the parish to serve his people, can better address how to match appropriate resources to its ministries and nurture good stewards. Thus, the parish will be able to offer people a more fervent and vibrant experience of God's love poured out in his Church. *Parish Finance: Best Practices in Church Management* should take its place alongside the best practical volumes we have for catechesis, sacramental preparation, education, and pastoral ministry—all in the service of God's holy Church.

May 27, 2016

Preface

Welcome to *Parish Finance: Best Practices in Church Management*. We are two dedicated Catholic laymen who are excited about this opportunity to contribute to the effective financial stewardship of our parishes and other Catholic organizational entities.

As parishioners, we've watched as our pastors have become overwhelmed in carrying out their threefold ministry of teaching, sanctifying, and governing. Our parishes have become larger and more complex. Many priests have been asked to pastor multiple parishes, and many of them, because of the priest shortage, find themselves the only priest assigned to a parish. While all three priestly functions require time and effort, it is clear that the governance function is where our pastors need the most assistance.

Let's be honest. Few if any men enter the priesthood because they want to run a small business. While a parish isn't a business per se, it has many of the trappings of a business, including the need for budgeting and financial management. In any event, church leaders have a stewardship responsibility to ensure that resources are used effectively. Frequently, this involves the use of sound budgeting and financial management, along with other skills (human resources, planning, etc.) typically associated with running a business.

Not only do most priests not have the natural inclination to carry out their governance function, they receive little or no training in it. Seminaries, overwhelmed with the requirements to educate their men in the skills necessary to become good priests, are unable to find room in the curriculum to train them to be pastors. This may not have been a severe problem in the past, when newly ordained priests could expect to spend ten to fifteen years as apprentices of sorts by serving as parochial vicars. However, today in many dioceses it is common for men to be assigned their first pastorate in as few as two years out of seminary.

Not only pastors face this problem. Many church employees, working in dioceses or social service agencies, find themselves thrust into managerial positions. Their backgrounds might be in theology, education, or social work. Now they find themselves managing, with little or no background in business.

For most pastors and church managers, financial management is among the more mystifying governance functions. It's probably fair to say that, until someone has gone through a budgeting cycle, become conversant with financial statements, or has had to make financial management decisions, the process can be intimidating. The purpose of this book is to take the anxiety out of those processes. Budgeting and financial management are not rocket science. As this book demonstrates, each activity can be broken down into a handful of component steps that follow one another logically. When viewed this way, the mystery of creating and monitoring a budget disappears, financial statements no longer appear to be written in Greek (although some pastors might prefer reading Greek to reading financial statements), and other financial management tools are no longer intimidating.

We have written this book for all whose ministry involves some degree of financial management, whether that person is a pastor, a parish business manager, a diocesan official, or a manager in a faith-based organization. Newcomers will find it especially useful, but even experienced church managers will appreciate the detail provided, as we take them step by step through the budget cycle (formulation, execution, and control); assist them in preventing fraud through the implementation of sound internal financial controls; provide a basic primer on running a capital campaign; and introduce tools like cost/benefit analysis and breakeven analysis that enhance their decision-making processes.

In writing this book, we stand on the shoulders of many who influenced and challenged our thinking. They start with Mike's mom and dad, Michele and Joe Castrilli, who taught him that anything is possible if he puts his heart and his mind into his passion. They also include Mike's teacher, Donna Eichenlaub, who taught him to study hard and to never stop learning, and his professors at Syracuse University's Maxwell School: Bill Duncombe, Bernard Jump, and Stuart Bretschneider, who inspired him to pursue his enthusiasm for budgeting and financial management. Chuck credits the late Dean Hoge of Catholic University and Jim Davidson of Purdue for their guidance over the years, and his wife, Ann, for her unwavering support.

Special thanks go to Kait Riggs Zech, CPA, who read parts of the manuscript and made significant contributions through her comments.

A debt of gratitude is owed to Donna Crilly, our editor at Paulist Press, who has been a constant source of encouragement and positive feedback, even as she turned our rough writing style into understandable English.

But we are most grateful to our devoted church managers, including pastors, parish business managers, diocesan officials, and all who work in faith-based organizations, who persevere in their efforts to be good stewards of the church's resources. It is to them that we dedicate this book.

Mike Castrilli
Chuck Zech

Introduction

Managing a parish has always been a challenge. Parish revenue is unsure, relying primarily on voluntary parishioner contributions through the collection basket. Facilities are frequently undermaintained as scarce resources go toward current mission. The labor force is composed of a large number of volunteers who need to be motivated. Staff is typically overworked and underpaid. And the person primarily responsible for the governance of the parish (along with teaching and sanctifying duties) is the pastor, who more than likely has received no formal training in any of this during his seminary days.

Managing a parish today is arguably more complicated, faced with more challenges and competing priorities, than any time in recent history. Many parishes, especially those in urban areas in the Northeast and Midwest, face declining membership. Others, notably those in many suburban areas and in the South and Midwest, are bulging at the seams. Parishes are becoming more multicultural. Parishes are unique; yet they face similar challenges. There are financial tensions, shortages of staff and volunteers—and the constant pressure to "do more with less." And yes, by the way, we have fewer priests to carry out this workload, resulting in men being asked to pastor larger, and increasingly multiple, parishes.

Church managers are busy addressing the variety of pastoral and spiritual needs of their parishioners. Understanding all aspects of parish operations can be staggering. Budgeting and parish finance can become a particularly overwhelming concept because of the variety of language, terms, and outcomes. Our goal in this book is to demystify financial concepts, educate you on methods and tactics you can use to plan and manage resources, and equip you with tools that can assist you along the way. This book is intended for any church manager, whether ordained or lay, wanting to learn more about budgets and finance.

Before we go any further, let's make it clear: *the Church is not a business*. But we do have a stewardship responsibility to use our resources effectively to carry out God's work on earth. Frequently, this responsibility requires us to employ sound business management techniques, including those concerned with budgeting and other aspects of parish finance.

> Stewardship involves guiding parishioners to recognize that all they have is really a gift from God, who asks them to return a portion of their time, talent, and treasure to support God's work on earth. Stewardship is not about something they do, but rather about who they are, and whose they are.
>
> As a community of faith, parish financial decisions should be centered on these same stewardship values. See Luke 19:11–26 and 2 Corinthians 9:6–13.

One might immediately think that any book about budget and finance is focused on "money." But this is not a book about money. Rather it is a guide for learning how to connect resources to achieve parish mission, vision, and goals. All of the principles, methods, tools, and tips in this book are centered on faith. Budget and financial management without prayer and discernment would be like building a ship and then realizing there is no rudder to steer, no engine for power, and no water to sail.

The Book's Goals and Objectives

The overarching goal of the book is to help you go from learning, to understanding, to implementing the concepts we discuss. We designed the book around the following objectives:

- **Practical** — Provide outcome-oriented solutions. The book not only teaches concepts but provides solutions for ministers on the go.
- **Accessible**—Clarify key terminology, offer easy-to-use templates, and turn "complex" concepts into action-oriented tools.
- **Best in Class**—Offer proven methods that provide the foundation for techniques and tactics that can be used in everyday situations.
- **Interactive**—Use examples throughout the book based on actual challenges and common questions relevant to parish life. The material is intended for readers to engage by practicing the concepts and trying out the tools.
- **Resourceful**—Provide readers meaningful resources for further study.

The Organization of the Book

The book is organized into three sections that connect the fundamental concepts of budgeting and financial management to helping parishes achieve their goals.

Section I: Budgeting: Aligning Resources to Parish Goals

Aligned to parish mission and vision, the budget is your blueprint to achieve parish priorities, goals, and objectives. This section offers a budget primer on fundamental concepts, discusses how to create a collaborative and transparent budget process, and walks through the step-by-step process of building a budget.

Section II: Budget Execution and Control

Many church managers believe that their work is completed once the budget has been developed. But formulating a budget is only the first step. As the fiscal year progresses, the budget needs to be executed and controls must be exerted. Executing the budget involves activities like budget apportionment (releasing funds at specific periods) and disbursing funds consistent with the budget outline. Controls include keeping the budget on track by regularly comparing actual revenue and spending with budgeted amounts and establishing internal financial controls to ensure the safe handling of funds.

Section III: Financial Management: Analysis, Insight, and Action

In this section, we introduce the reader to parish financial reporting and to financial analysis tools that assist in decision making, along with fundraising techniques for conducting capital campaigns.

Even after the budget has been created and executed, and all controls are in place, the church manager's work is still not done. Financial statements need to be prepared for reporting the parish's financial condition to the diocese and other stakeholders. Parish decision making on programmatic matters can be vastly improved by the use of some basic financial analysis tools. And it is only a matter of time until a parish needs to conduct a capital campaign to maintain or expand its facilities.

St. Michael's Parish Case Study

As a way to introduce each topic, the guide follows the trials and tribulations of a hypothetical Fr. Dave, a newly appointed pastor. At the start of each chapter, we provide a summary for what Fr. Dave will learn and, in the process, the concepts and principles that we will discuss.

Introduction to Fr. Dave

Fr. Dave is at a crossroads. He has been blessed by a new opportunity—but with it come new and unfamiliar challenges. He is a diocesan priest, just beginning his first assignment as a pastor. He loves the spiritual ministry of his work—but he's finding much more is now expected from him.

Fr. Dave is four years out of seminary. During his formation, he learned much about what it takes to be a successful priest, but he learned virtually nothing about what it takes to be a successful pastor. His seminary did not offer a single course on parish administration, leaving him in the dark on many basic financial and operational issues. Those issues also never came up during his formation or in spiritual direction. It seems everyone assumed he would be introduced to "pastoring" during the early years of his priesthood.

Unfortunately, when Fr. Dave was a parochial vicar, the senior priest controlled nearly every element of parish operations. Fr. Dave was not included in many of his pastoring duties, like talks with the parish business manager or meetings with the parish finance council. Even after several years in the parish, Fr. Dave did not know much more about the administrative side of pastoring than he had when he started.

But God had plans for Fr. Dave. When one of the diocese's pastors died unexpectedly, the bishop had no choice but to appoint Fr. Dave as pastor of a midsize parish—in spite of his obvious lack of preparation. The stakes are high: his new parish needs some significant financial cleanup, and construction drafts are already in the works to renovate the parish hall.

This new role will involve much more than the prayer, homilies, and parishioner visits he so enjoys. Fr. Dave is now an administrator and a manager, faced with the legal and fiduciary responsibilities that come with financial oversight. It's certainly not how he planned it—but Fr. Dave quickly realizes that he will have to learn to be a pastor through on-the-job training.

St. Michael's Parish Profile

St. Michael's Parish is a medium-sized parish of 1,300 families in a suburban setting. The parish operates with a skeletal staff: a receptionist/secretary (Edith), a director of faith formation (Michele), a director of music (Ron), a maintenance manager (Joe), and a part-time business manager (Mary). Mary was hired because she is a dedicated and trustworthy parishioner, but she has no business background. The previous pastor and Mary relied on common sense—rather than structured business plans—to manage the parish.

Figure 0-1
St. Michael's staff

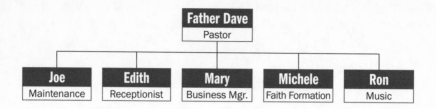

Summary

A key differentiator between churches and other organizations is the importance of prayer, discernment, and formation in order to understand and prioritize the future. There are a number of elements that can be used as strategy around discernment.

Christifideles Laici clearly frames the parish at the center of church life. Pope John Paul II writes, "The ecclesial community, while always having a universal dimension, finds its most immediate and visible expression in the *parish*. This is where the Church is seen locally. In a certain sense, it is the *Church living in the midst of the homes of her sons and daughters*. It is necessary that in light of the faith all rediscover the true meaning of the parish, that is, the place where the very 'mystery' of the Church is present and at work, even if at times it is lacking persons and means."[1]

As you read the book, keep the following principles in mind:

- Prayer, discernment, and collaboration are central to these topics.

- Before undertaking budget planning and financial management, ensure that current needs and opportunities at the parish have been discussed and assessed. An effective pastoral planning process will lead to answering questions like the following: *Where are we today as it relates to our mission and vision? What are our strengths, weaknesses, opportunities, and risks? Where do we see ourselves into the future?* The answers to these questions form the basis for connecting resources to priorities.

- We recognize that all concepts are not one-size-fits-all solutions. However, by learning the methods, you can apply these techniques to the unique aspects of your parish organization.

- Faith in God, through his Son Jesus Christ, is the center of all mission and ministry and the glue binding these concepts together.

The reason this topic gets us so excited is that when resources are tied to priorities, visions become reality. Once people see budgeting as an opportunity to align, execute, and deliver on the wide variety of goals that a parish establishes, the budget becomes a resource, and not a document intended to punish poor financial managers.

1. John Paul II, *Christifideles Laici* (Vatican City: Libreria Editrice Vaticana, 1988), no. 26.

Section I

Budgeting

Aligning Resources to Parish Goals

Chapter 1

Getting Started with Parish Budgeting

Chapter 1 Preview

In this chapter, we help Fr. Dave to do the following:

- Define what a budget is and how it connects to parish priorities
- Learn key benefits of budgeting
- Recognize the need for a collaborative and transparent budget process
- Identify and understand the budget lifecycle phases
  - Phase 1: Budget formulation (develop)
  - Phase 2: Budget execution (implement)
  - Phase 3: Budget control (stay on track)

St. Michael's Parish—Fr. Dave: "Where Do I Begin?"

It took all the faith he could muster, but Fr. Dave accepted the appointment to lead St. Michael's. Coming into a parish where the beloved pastor has recently died leaves him big shoes to fill. And my, how different things are here!

In his first few weeks on the job, there has been much to learn, from the names of his new parishioners to the maze-like layout of this new complex. Every time he goes to the restroom, he makes a wrong turn. One afternoon, while sitting at his new desk, the architect called to speak to him about sketches for the renovations to the parish hall. He was so confused, he told the architect he'd have to find an answer and return the call at another time. Everything feels just a bit overwhelming.

Then, early one morning, the parish finance chair called. "When should we expect to meet?" she asked. Fr. Dave was caught by surprise—meet about what, he wondered. "I know you only started three weeks ago, so I guess you don't yet know our process," she continued. "We need to send in our final budget to the diocese in six weeks. You should ask Mary how much work has already been done on it."

When Fr. Dave spoke to Mary, the situation went from unsettling to downright nerve-rattling: no work had been done on a budget that's due in a month and a half! "No," she says, "the previous pastor would just outline regular expenses and increase the total collection amount by 1 percent. Then, I'd go back and make sure the numbers worked. We usually started right around now. But come to think of it—this year will probably be more complicated with the renovations to the parish hall and new program ideas from the staff."

It was frightening, to say the least.

The clock is now ticking for Fr. Dave's budget deadline—and the responsibility to his parish and to the diocese rests squarely on his shoulders!

Budget Anxiety

If you are like Fr. Dave, when you hear the words *budget* or *budget process*, a feeling of anxiety may come over you. If so, you are not alone. The worry may come in the form of confusion over terminology, requirements for calculating projected income and expenses, or the limited time you have to dedicate to the process. If you have limited experience with budgeting, you may feel overwhelmed and fear that whatever is created will be used as a measure and punishment against a program, your management, or both.

Our goal is to take anxiety and fear out of the budget process. We hope to make budgeting something to enjoy, rather than dread. We will discuss budgeting best practices, guidelines, and tools, and bring them together to help you determine what you need to complete to prepare, create, communicate, present, and manage the parish budget. We will also discuss strategies to help you engage and collaborate with staff, parishioners, the local community, and your archdiocese or diocese.

Budget Defined

Let's start with some fundamental concepts and terminology. Budgets can be large or small, include a high or low number of categories of money coming in and resources going out, but all budgets highlight a list of priorities. A **budget** is defined as *the planning and management tool for executing priorities by projecting, allocating, and managing the money you receive and the money you plan to spend.* Important questions that we will help you address include the following:

1. How will you engage with the parish staff, the congregation, and other stakeholders to establish your priorities?

2. What assumptions have you built into your plan?

3. How can you most accurately allocate the resources you expect to receive and spend?

Without getting caught up in the numbers yet, let's address the question, "How can budgeting help achieve goals, your priorities, and manage your organization effectively?

The Benefits of Budgeting

What are the key benefits of this process? This is worth taking a few minutes to review. This is where budgeting benefits you and your organization in more ways than one!

The budget is the *plan* and *tool* that will help you

1. Connect resources to parish priorities

2. Create a plan to allocate money coming into the parish and expenses to be paid

3. Ensure that plans stay on track

4. Empower effective financial decisions

5. Bring collaboration, communication, and buy-in

6. Strategize for the future

1. Connect Resources to Parish Priorities

Connecting parish priorities to available resources is one of the greatest advantages to developing a budget. Show me your budget and I can tell you how you spend your time, where you focus your resources, and what you believe are the greatest priorities for your parish and programs.

Think about your personal spending. If you showed us your latest bank statement or credit card bills, we would be able to tell you how you spend your time and where you focus your personal resources. All we would have to do is take your income and expenses for the statement period and assign categories to the ones we see repeated. For example, we may see expenses for great restaurants (dining), a gym membership (fitness), doctor visits or medications (medical), and ticket purchases for shows and concerts (entertainment). On the incoming side, we may see a check deposit from your job (salary). If you provided two or three months of data, we would have a good idea about how you prioritize resources.

The same can be said of your parish priorities. What are the categories of income and spending that the parish receives and spends? Most likely, the largest income category for the parish includes offertory collections, while staff salary and benefits drive the majority of expenses. These categories make sense as priorities. Without collection income, the parish would have virtually no resources to operate besides savings or any endowments. Salary and benefits also make sense because of the need for the most critical resource for any organization—people to accomplish the work.

2. Create a Plan to Allocate Money Coming into the Parish and Expenses Paid

The budget is the plan for how you will allocate money coming into the parish and expenses you will pay. Incoming money may include weekly collections; stole fees for baptisms, weddings, and funerals; fees paid for religious education; and special collections. The parish also has expenses—for example, staff salary and benefits, utilities for the various parish facilities (church, rectory, parish hall), and a variety of other expenses (office supplies, copying fees, website hosting, etc.). Without a plan, there is no roadmap to ensure that each month you have enough money to pay the bills and adequate resources available in case something goes wrong.

3. Ensure That Plans Stay on Track

The effective allocation of resources leads to the next advantage of budgeting, helping you stay on track. Let's face it, as church managers, you know that circumstances change, events happen, staff leave, and programs change. The budget is like a GPS in your car. The GPS provides verbal and visual cues on your progress to your destination. It also lets you know when you make a wrong turn. In the same way, the budget roadmap provides benefits. "Have we received what we expected in terms of income?" "Are we on track with our spending?" "Has something come up that we didn't expect?" The budget will help answer all of these questions and ensure that if you made a wrong turn, you can still get back on course.

4. Empower Effective Financial Decisions

The budget provides the freedom for you to make solid financial decisions. It puts parameters around how much you expect to spend and receive. However, as circumstances change, the budget is a guiding document to ensure that we clearly see how decisions that are made impact other elements or categories. The budget can quickly show you the tradeoffs.

The budget empowers effective decision making by providing a guide for saying yes or no as circumstances arise. The budget can give you freedom to know the answers to questions like, "Do we have enough money to buy LED televisions for the CCD classrooms?" "Do we have extra money for a new vacation bible school?"

5. Bring Collaboration, Communication, and Buy-In

When it comes to budgeting, collaboration and communication leads to **buy-in**. Collaboration allows you to dialogue with your staff, the various councils, and the congregation. Without input, the budget loses all of the other benefits listed above because it does not reflect parish priorities and bring stakeholders together to form a united front when it comes to managing money.

The Answer Is Collaboration!

- What are the priorities for your organization?
- How do you achieve buy-in for the financial plan for the parish?
- How do you get those interested in success of parish programs?

Collaboration is the glue that provides information and insights that cannot be achieved by one individual. Collaboration paired with open communication is where the budget will help church managers achieve the greatest potential of their organization.

---

6. Strategize for the Future

The budget is also forward looking, not merely a document that is pulled off the shelf once a year to be developed and approved by the finance committee. The budget will be used not only to look at the present but also to plan for the future, whether it is deciding to save a specific percentage of money for a future capital asset purchase (an asset used for more than one year), ensuring that there is money set aside in case of emergency, or funding a specific future initiative (new organ, parish hall renovation), and so forth.

Even with all of these advantages, creating a budget may still seem overwhelming. Let's break down the process into manageable components.

Overview of Budget Process and Lifecycle
Designing a Collaborative and Transparent Budget Process

Understanding is the first step to any budget process. It is critical to begin by developing one that is collaborative and transparent. As we noted above, collaboration has numerous advantages. Transparency is a commitment to openness in process, methods, and decisions.

Some leaders think that when making financial decisions, it is better to keep the budget a secret or not reveal details to others. Actually, the opposite is true. Without a transparent, collaborative, and open budget process, it is far more likely that when difficult choices arise, the stakeholders without knowledge of the budget will be less likely to support difficult trade-offs. Transparency will lead to a process that is efficient and will ensure that you don't have to reinvent the wheel each year when you undertake the budget.

People often make the budget process into an arduous task, but it doesn't have to be overly complex. You can use the budget framework we propose to create something transparent, repeatable, efficient, and effective in leading parish financial management.

The Budget Lifecycle

The **budget lifecycle** is the roadmap to help guide you as the parish budget is developed. As figure 1-1 displays, the budget lifecycle includes three phases that build upon one another: budget formulation, execution, and control.

Figure 1-1
Budget lifecycle phases

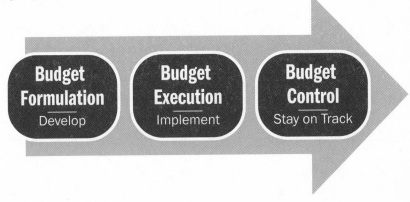

Phase 1: Budget Formulation (Develop)

Budget formulation is the process used to develop the budget. This is where you will review the variety of income and expense categories and determine how much you expect to receive and project how much you plan to spend. There are a variety of methods we can use to create the budget and in which we can develop the budget. Whether you use top-down, bottom-up, incremental, or flexible budgeting, the framework will help you structure the development.

In the budget formulation phase, the parish will get into the nuts and bolts of budget building. Here a variety of questions will be answered, including the following:

- What are the assumptions and expectations for the upcoming year?
- How will resources be allocated for staff, programs, emerging requirements, or assets?
- What information and methods will be used to ensure that accurate projections and forecasts are developed for income and expenses?

This is the phase of the budget process where we will build the "budget house." We will review architecture plans, pour a solid foundation, frame the walls, and build a strong roof so that as storms rage, the house remains sturdy and strong.

Phase 2: Budget Execution (Implement)

Once the income and expense parameters have been set and the budget has been approved, the plan is ready to be implemented. **Budget execution** is the phase in the budget lifecycle when the checks are written, salaries paid, and income is received. Policies and procedures are established to ensure accountability. Clear roles and responsibilities are developed for who, what, when, and how resources will be authorized, distributed, and accounted for. The outcomes of this phase are policies and procedures for collecting and distributing resources.

Phase 3: Budget Control (Stay on Track)

Complementing the execution phase, budget control is the part of the budgeting lifecycle that ensures that the efforts that you have put into the other steps of the process are successful. Strategies and techniques can be deployed to keep you on track and headed in the right direction with warnings along the way if you are getting off track. Actual income and spending amounts are compared to budgeted projections to measure variances between the amounts. With this information, parish managers can accurately account for resources or deploy mitigation tactics if spending is getting out of control or if resources need to be reallocated.

All three of these phases build upon one another and create a budget lifecycle that brings flexibility, adaptability, and accountability to financial planning and actions.

Chapter Summary

The parish budget is the tool that connects financial resources to parish priorities. Not only will budgeting enable you to project, allocate, and manage resources effectively, it will empower you with information and insights to help inform decision making. Through a collaborative budget process and a phased approach to the budget lifecycle (formulation, execution, and control), the resources entrusted to the parish will be managed with ease and efficiency.

In chapter 2, we'll introduce and break down key budget terms and concepts to make these fundamental components of budgeting practical and accessible.

Chapter 2

Budget Fundamentals

Chapter 2 Preview

In this chapter, we help Fr. Dave to do the following:

- Understand basic budget terminology—budget size, categories, and assumptions
- Learn the structure and component parts of the parish master budget
  - Operating budget, income, and expenses
  - Capital budget and long-term asset planning
  - Parish accounts and investments
- Use the parish mission and vision statements as the foundation of the budget

St. Michael's Parish—Budget 101

Fr. Dave has never prepared a budget from scratch before. In fact, when he was an associate pastor, he had never even reviewed the budget! Where can he possibly begin? Mary was able to pull up the previous years' parish budgets, along with some bank statements. But many of the terms on the past budgets seem like a foreign language. Mary tells him, "Our operating budget is about $750,000. We have $110,726 in our checking account, $425,000 in deposits with the diocese and $50,000 in savings. The money we have with the diocese includes money available for our capital budget of about $191,453."

The numbers make his head spin. What about the new expenses? And how should he factor in that sky-high hourly rate quoted by the architect for the parish hall job?

Budget Primer—From Intimidating to Accessible

Many treasurers, financial managers, and other professionals familiar with budgeting and finances assume that everyone knows what they mean when they use terms that they consider common. Experts will talk about operating and capital budgets, restricted and unrestricted assets, chart of accounts, balance sheet, statement of cash flows...and the list goes on. The terminology can seem confusing. In the next chapters, we will discuss these items in depth, but why wait to get some quick definitions? Our goal is to take *intimidating* out of the conversation and replace it with *accessible*.

Budget Size

Those new to budgeting may become concerned over the "size" of their budget. You'll hear remarks such as,

- "That budget is huge!"
- "$100,000 is a small amount, don't worry too much."
- "No need for a budget process. When we run into trouble, we dip into the 'reserve fund.'"

The point is, it doesn't matter if your budget is $100,000, $10,000,000, or $100,000,000, budget size is relative to what you are trying to accomplish. Regardless of the number of zeroes, the concepts we will discuss apply to all budgets! Once you have the concepts down, you'll be in great shape to adjust your budget to fit your organization's needs.

Budget Categories

Budget categories are the classifications for the money that is received, money spent, and money saved. As we will see, categories also come in all shapes and sizes. The goal is to break down the budget into manageable chunks. This will help you plan, create, and manage your budget to ensure that you stay on track.

The good news is that budget methods, income and expense forecasting techniques, and budget development tactics can be used to create all elements of this comprehensive budget.

Never developed a budget? Have no fear!

To begin, write down your answers to these three questions:

1. What are the categories of money that you **plan to receive?**
   Examples: Sunday collections? Stole fees? Stewardship pledges? Tuition?

2. What are the categories for how you **spend money?**
   Examples: Salary and benefits? Office supplies? Copier costs?
   Maintenance costs related to the church or the rectory?

3. What **types of accounts** do you have?
   Examples: Checking account? Savings account? Investment account?

Budget Assumptions

Assumptions underlie all types of budgets. These are the expectations, predictions, and projections that will form the foundation for your budget. Budget assumptions help you outline and document what you expect in terms of income, expenses, and anything else that may affect your financial planning. It is critical to keep a list of the assumptions you use to create your budget. You can return to them often to determine whether your expectations were correct and make adjustments as necessary.

Many assumptions are based on past financial information, and these will help us inform the future. Here are some questions you might ask:

- Based on our weekly donations this year, how much can we expect to receive in the weekly collections?
- How much have we spent on utilities (e.g., gas, electric) this past year?
- What events will take place in this upcoming year that may have not occurred previously?

As you can see, some "guesstimating" is needed as you create the budget. Do not let this concern you—as we will see repeatedly, some areas of the budget process are more of an art than a science. The key is to use these principles as an advantage in the budget process. It can even be fun to make predictions about the future and then return to them to see if you were right or wrong! Whatever happens, it will help inform future actions, and you can make adjustments.

Overview of the Master Budget

There are a variety of ways to develop a budget, but we like to structure the system into what we call a master budget. The **master budget** will provide a consolidated view of both the operating and capital budgets for the parish. Income and expense projections along with a comprehensive list of budget assumptions are also included.

Figure 2-1
The master budget overview

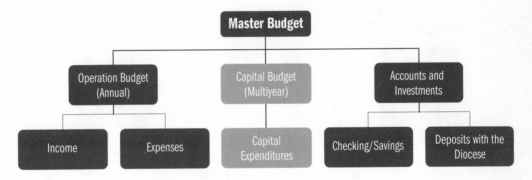

Operating Budget

The **operating budget** addresses the day-to-day *income* and *expenses* of managing the parish. This is the plan for projecting how much money is expected into the parish (*income*) and how much money will be spent (*expenses*). The budget is typically a twelve-month plan. The term **fiscal year** (abbreviated **FY**) is used to describe a twelve-month period for which an organization plans the use of funds and reports financial status. This may be a calendar year but can be any twelve-month period. Most parish budgets begin on July 1 and end on June 30.

Have you ever wondered why most parishes—and many nonprofits—use July 1 as the start of their fiscal year, instead of January 1, the day the calendar year begins? The answer to the question is quite simple. What is the busiest time of year for most parishes and nonprofits? The holidays! Whether one is a nonprofit collecting end-of-year donations or a church preparing for Christmas, December and January are typically a very busy time. Therefore, the summer months are good chance for parishes to finalize their budget, report their financial position, and begin a new accounting period.

Within the operating budget, let's briefly review operating income and expense categories.

Operating Income

Operating income is the money received from parishioners, donors, programs, and other streams (interest/subsidies) for the day-to-day functioning of the parish.

Some sample operating income categories include the following:

- Collections: Sunday, Holy Day, parish needs collections
- Liturgical and sacramental income
- Stole fees, novena, votive collections
- Bulletin, publications, gift store, rental income
- Development income
- Subsidies and grants
- Account interest

Table 2-1 displays the operating income categories at St. Michael's. Please note that archdiocesan/diocesan financial policies will dictate the specific categories for your parish. The categories listed on the following page are illustrative, but highlight typical categories for parishes.

Table 2-1
St. Michael's operating income categories

Line Item	Category
1000 Collections	
1001	Sunday Collections
1002	Holy Day Collections
1003	Parish Needs Collections
1100 Donations	
1101	Stole (Baptism, Weddings, Funerals)
1102	Flowers
1103	Candles
1200 Programs	
1201	Religious Education
1202	Adult Education
1203	Parish Picnic
1300 Other Income	
1301	Church Bulletin Advertising/Misc.
1302	Sales of Literature/Goods
1303	Interest and Dividends

Operating Expenses

Operating expenses are categories of everyday costs required to keep the parish running smoothly. Some sample expense categories include the following:

- Salaries
- Payroll tax and worker's compensation
- Health benefits/retirement
- Utilities
- Administrative costs
- Office and technology
- Liturgical and sacramental

As you can see from the income and expense categories, line item numbers (2000, 2100, 2200) are associated with each category of the budget. These numbers will assist in entering transactions and reporting financial information.

Table 2-2
St. Michael's operating expense categories

Line Item	Category	Line Item	Category
2000 Personnel/Salaries		2300 Administrative/Office (continued)	
2001	Pastor	2315	Interest and Bank Charges
2002	Business Manager	2316	Criminal Background Checks
2003	Secretary	2317	Contracted Services
2004	Music	2318	Extra Clergy Assistance
2005	Faith Formation	2319	Fundraising
2006	Maintenance Manager	2320	Parish Hall Supplies
2100 Personnel/Other		2400 Liturgical/Sacramental	
2101	Lay Medical Insurance	2401	Liturgical Supplies
2102	Clergy Insurance	2402	Flowers
2103	Employer Social Security	2403	Vestments
2104	Employer Medicare	2404	Liturgical Seasons
2105	Lay Employee Retirement	2405	Sacramental Supplies (Baptism, Confirmation, etc.)
2106	Workers' Comp. and Disability	2406	Music Program
2107	Unemployment Insurance	2407	Music Publications
2108	ADP Payroll Expense	2500 Programs	
2109	Retreats and Workshops	2501	RCIA
2110	Lay Training	2502	Religious Education
2111	Associations/Membership	2503	Adult Faith Formation
2112	Gifts and Bonuses	2504	Young Adults
2200 Diocesan		2505	Vacation Bible School
2201	Diocesan Assessment	2506	Parish Events
2300 Administrative/Office		2507	Parish Picnic
2301	Supplies and Equipment	2508	Evangelization
2302	Postage	2509	Social Justice Programs
2303	Printing and Copying	2510	Councils and Committees
2304	Offertory Envelopes	2600 Plant/Facilities	
2305	Advertising	2601	Water and Sewer
2306	Audit and Legal Services	2602	Electric
2307	Security System	2603	Building Supplies
2308	Internet	2604	Regular Building Maintenance
2309	Office Phones	2605	Building Repairs
2310	Cell Phones	2606	Pest and Termite Control
2311	Website Support and Development	2607	Grounds Maintenance
2312	Automobile and Travel	2608	Equipment Repair
2313	Priest Reimbursement	2609	Real Estate Taxes
2314	Parish Meals and Hosting	2610	Property and Liability Insurance

Capital Budget

Parishes may also have a budget specifically designed around **capital assets**. The capital budget includes money available for **assets** (items that have value) that extend beyond the year that they were purchased or used for services. Unlike the operating budget, which has a shorter or more immediate-term focus, the capital budget focuses on the long term.

For parishes, the best examples of capital assets are the church building and the rectory. The use of both of these facilities will go far beyond one year.

The **capital budget** is the resourcing plan for updating, repairing, maintaining, or purchasing assets whose value extends beyond a one-year window. You can also think of the capital budget as resource planning for future big-ticket purchases or renovation. Examples might include the purchase of a new organ, paving the parking lot, or a fund to address emergencies like a roof caving in. The period associated with this component of the master budget typically extends beyond twelve months and may extend two to five years or more.

Table 2-3 displays the current capital budget categories at St. Michael's. Funds for these expenditures have been set aside in previous years and put into a reserve account (think savings!). This money is available for use by St. Michael's for expenses related to these categories.

Table 2-3
St. Michael's capital budget categories

Line Item	Category
3000 Capital Expenditures	
3001	Parish Hall Renovations
3002	Parking Lot Upgrades
3003	Church Improvements
3004	Rectory Improvements
3005	Equipment/Furniture
3006	Sound System Upgrade

Parish Accounts and Investments

The parish will have a series of accounts to be included in the master budget. These may be checking, savings, and investment accounts. Archdiocesan/diocesan policies will dictate the guidelines related to the types of accounts and investments a parish can deploy. Table 2-4 displays the accounts at St. Michael's.

Table 2-4
St. Michael's accounts

Line Item	Category
4000 Parish Accounts	
4001	Checking Account
4002	Deposits with the Diocese
4003	Savings Account
4004	Other Investments

Donations

When reading through parish financial documents, you may also see a number of fund types. Particularly with donations, you may see the words *restricted* or *unrestricted funds*. Don't let the words intimidate you. A *restricted donation* or *fund* is simply income received that has been designated for a specific purpose and can ONLY be used for that specific purpose. For example, a parishioner donates ten thousand dollars for a new scholarship fund at the school. The money would then be called "restricted" because the donor's intent is to have the money used only for the purposes that she has designated. An *unrestricted donation* can be used for any purposes at the parish.

Connecting Parish Mission, Vision, and Goals

As noted in the introduction, the foundation of the budget is the alignment of resources to the parish mission, vision, and goals. In chapter 1, we saw that the budget determines how limited time and money will be spent throughout a given period. Underlying all components of the master budget is how the budget aligns with the parish's priorities. Often the parish mission, vision, and strategic goals and objectives contain elements of these priorities. If you have a current parish mission statement, vision statement, or strategic plan, pull out these documents. Our goal in the next chapters is to design a process and build a budget that centers on delivering and achieving parish priorities by aligning parish resources with those goals.

Chapter Summary

If you want to understand budgeting, you must be comfortable with the terms and concepts. If you learn the relative simplicity of the definitions of critical terms such as *master budget*, *operating income and expenses*, *capital budgeting*, and *parish accounts and investments*, you will demystify budgeting. When you link the budget to parish mission, vision, and goals, you're off to a great start. Now that you have been introduced to key elements of budgeting, you are armed with the information you need to take the next step.

In chapter 3, we will take these foundational principles, apply them, and establish a budget process that is collaborative and transparent.

Chapter 3

Designing a Collaborative and Transparent Budget Process

Chapter 3 Preview

In this chapter, we help Fr. Dave to do the following:

- Learn how collaboration brings freedom to the budget process
- Understand the budget calendar, activities, and milestones
- Go in depth on the budget formulation stages
  - Establish priorities
  - Deliver guidance
  - Develop preliminary budget
  - Gain feedback and finalize
- Learn tips to get started with the budget process

St. Michael's Parish—Budget Processes

The parish's budget clock is ticking, and there is no time to waste! Fr. Dave realizes that many of his new parishioners—and the diocesan leaders who put him in this post—see this budget as his first big test.

Fr. Dave knows one thing: he won't be able to do this alone, and he doesn't want to. The more he talks to Mary, the more he realizes that the previous pastor allocated the parish's money without much input. The pastor did the budget in secret—and then passed it along to the parish finance council for their rubber stamp.

This year, Fr. Dave wants to budget in a spirit of collaboration and transparency. What's more, he doesn't want to make a mistake! And he knows that on a project like this, input from his in-house "experts" on the finance and pastoral councils will help catch errors before the budget makes it to his bishop's desk.

Fr. Dave knows that there are probably as many opinions on how to spend parish money as there are parishioners. He wants everyone to have a voice—but he knows that too many cooks will spoil the broth! How can he get the parish's input effectively? How can he translate their ideas and goals into a plan that will work financially?

Budget Process Essentials

When creating an effective budget process, sometimes the critical first step is left out of the process: commitment to collaboration and open communication. Whether this means your parish staff, the finance council, parishioners, or diocesan officials, when you involve multiple stakeholders early in the budget process, the benefits are enormous when you begin using the budget as a tool to help you make decisions. It is much easier for individuals to validate decisions when they know what opportunities and constraints are included because they have been involved throughout the process.

It is tempting for parish leaders to convince themselves that it is more expedient to keep the budget a secret or not let others into the details. This can be very damaging. A parish without a transparent, collaborative, and open budget process will likely learn that when difficult decisions need to be made regarding financial matters, stakeholders who have had no input into the budget are less likely to support difficult trade-offs.

How do you create an open budget process? First, it is very important to set expectations. If you are the leader and establish priorities for the upcoming year, have you communicated these priorities? There is nothing more frustrating for a staff than to have an "open process," only to have their ideas steamrolled in the end because the leader would never fund a certain initiative.

An open process involves communicating expectations up front, letting people know any funding constraints, or discussing directly what is on and off the table for the upcoming year. Being direct and open during this phase of the budget process saves an enormous amount of frustration for everyone. One option is to hold a meeting with your staff when you begin the budget process so you can brainstorm ideas or discuss initiatives for the upcoming year.

If you are asking staff to submit new program ideas or details for ongoing projects, have you provided guidance in terms of how they are to develop the cost figures or narrative? Be sure to provide direction and make your expectations clear. When the staff buys into the budget, they will also help manage it. The budget becomes part of the culture. People know that a budget is a living document and that if they are going to request additional resources or need something new, they are an integral link to other departments and staff.

The Budget Formulation Stages

Budget formulation is the process used to develop resource planning estimates for income and spending categories for a given period. As we discussed in chapter 2, for church organizations, budget formulation can span a few months or a few weeks. Formulation can also occur on multiple levels. For example, as a diocese prepares the overall diocesan budget, parishes within the diocese are also undergoing their own budget processes to compile the data and information needed for their operating and capital budget submissions to the pastor, finance council, and the community at large.

Whether you have a budget from previous years or you are starting from scratch, these steps can help you to identify and strategize what you need to do to get this budget completed.

Let's walk through examples of various budget formulation stages that you may develop or expand at your organization.

Figure 3-1
Budget formulation stages

Stage 1: Establish Priorities

Include in your budget process time to brainstorm and establish budget priorities. This is when you meet with staff, parishioners, or other stakeholders and encourage the process of formulating ideas. It is a great time to build a spirit of collaboration. Determine who should be involved in preparation of the various components of your budget. Who will develop new program proposals? Who can help with estimated costs?

Timing: approx. 4–5 months prior to the budget being finalized

Stage 2: Deliver Guidance

Develop a document (one or two pages) outlining your expectations of those from whom you are requesting information. Include guidance for developing cost estimates, proposing new programs, or justifying resources. There should be no guessing games regarding what you are looking at in estimates. Most income and expense estimates contain uncertainty anyway, so take that anxiety out of the creation of the budget. For example, if you have a budget target in mind, tell people. If not, then say so. If you have been thinking about canceling a program or initiative, let those involved know your thought process so they have the opportunity to discuss it with you. People want direct feedback. No one wants to complete a proposal only to find out that the program was not even being considered. These types of budget "paper exercises" will only undermine your leadership and dissatisfy those working with you. Expectation setting may be challenging to deliver in the moment, but honesty saves everyone time and aggravation, and helps you achieve respect during the next budget cycle and for your leadership. Allow adequate time for estimates and justifications to be produced.

Timing: approx. 4 months prior to the budget being finalized

Stage 3: Develop Preliminary Budget

Stage 3 is when your team estimates parish income and expenses, designs program budgets, and creates performance goals. Using your parish financial software and other tools at your disposal, you will be able to consolidate information so you can review the various budget elements (income, expenses, and program justifications) from different perspectives. Many archdiocesan/diocesan policies specify which software program each parish is expected or required to use. Learn more by reviewing the financial policies of your archdiocese/diocese. When the information is in this type of format, you will have a broader perspective and visibility of the various components that will make up your budget.

Timing: approx. 2 months prior to the budget being finalized

Stage 4: Gain Feedback and Finalize

Share the budget with those you have involved from the earliest phases of the process. After you have a draft budget, include stakeholders by allowing them to give you feedback as you prepare your final proposal. Consistent information sharing will continue to build momentum and ultimate buy-in for the creation of a collaborative budget. Buy-in at this stage is defined as ownership and understanding of the budget among stakeholders who are critical for the achievement of your policies and programs. In a parish, this includes staff, parishioners, finance and pastoral councils, and others who help you achieve success.

Timing: approx. 1 month prior to the budget being finalized

Transparency in how the budget is formulated, transferability of the process from year to year, and the building of a collaborative environment are just a few of the key benefits for this type of staged approach.

Figure 3-2
Sample budget formulation calendar

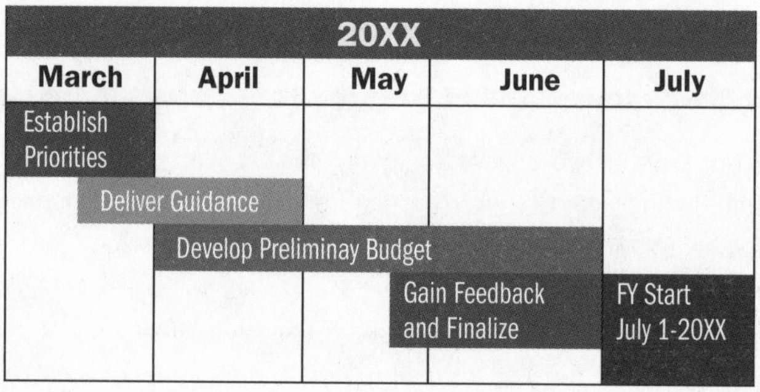

20XX				
March	**April**	**May**	**June**	**July**
Establish Priorities				
	Deliver Guidance			
		Develop Preliminay Budget		
			Gain Feedback and Finalize	FY Start July 1-20XX

Quick Tips for Getting Started with the Budgeting Process

Following are some practical suggestions and reflection questions as you look to implement these components in your organization.

Establish a Process (Even If It Is Not Perfect)

The first year of any new process can be challenging, but once established, every part of the organization will understand what is expected. For example, if your budget begins on July 1, you may want to establish that budget guidance will be distributed each April and a draft budget will be proposed by Memorial Day. Developing a schedule of key budget process dates provides everyone more flexibility so they can effectively manage their time. Establish a process in year one with the knowledge that it may not be perfect and that you can refine it by year two.

Provide Clear Guidance

Give clear guidance on your expectations for the process, the future, and what success looks like moving forward. If you are going to ask others for information, communicate your objectives and give visibility in your thinking for the upcoming year.

Open Communication and Stakeholder Involvement

Keep the budget process open and enable all voices to be heard. Hold a town hall-style meeting and welcome all parishioners when you open the budget process for the upcoming year and set expectations. Listen to the voices of the people around you. Open up the priority-setting process so you can gain broader involvement and commitment from those in your organization. Ask individuals to help brainstorm, but if not, be clear about the direction you are setting. When others feel involved, they will be more committed.

Chapter Summary

The budget process can be broken down into manageable stages in order to make this process clear, collaborative, and transparent. Information sharing with staff and parishioners allows the parish community to rally and buy into shared goals and objectives. By establishing clear priorities, delivering guidance on targets and expectations, and then developing a preliminary budget that incorporates all of these elements, you are on track to deliver an effective resource plan. Once feedback is obtained, the budget is finalized and ready for implementation.

Now that we have discussed the budget process, let's turn process into action. In chapter 4, we will discuss how to build the budget step by step.

Chapter 4

Budget Formulation Part I

Establishing a Framework

Chapter 4 Preview

In this chapter, we help Fr. Dave to do the following:

- Gather pastoral documents, policies, and information to assist in the budget formulation phase
- Collect information from current and past budgets
- Learn the high-level methods for developing budgets
  - Top-down budgeting
  - Bottom-up or zero-based budgeting
  - Incremental budgeting
- Apply methods to parish programs

St. Michael's Parish—Let's Build the Budget

As Fr. Dave continues his education, he quickly learns that this budget will be a financial outline for his entire first year in the parish, setting priorities and establishing a framework to carry out the parish's mission. But what exactly are those priorities? What is most important to the parishioners? What expenditures does this group feel are critical to doing the work of the Lord?

It's obvious that this is about more than just paying the electric and heating bills. This budget will be about establishing a plan—and somehow, Fr. Dave needs to make sure that the budget actually reflects the vision of his parishioners.

The process only got more complicated when he began asking parishioners for basic input. He hoped they would offer guidance. Instead, they offered new projects and new plans. It seems everyone has an idea for new ways the parish's money can be spent. How should he consider each of those proposals? And what should he make of all of it?

Prepare for Takeoff

To reduce some of the stress that accompanies compiling an effective budget, we recommend that Fr. Dave collect some data. Consider an airplane preparing for departure. Prior to leaving the gate, the pilot and copilot go through a series of preflight checklists. Together they review and confirm that all of the plane's instruments and controls are in working order so that they can arrive safely at their destination. These standard procedures ensure that nothing is missed. Fr. Dave can deploy the same strategy. What elements does he need in his checklist to ensure that he delivers an effective budget?

Parish Documentation—Mission/Vision/Strategic Plans

As noted previously, as he approaches the budgeting process, Fr. Dave should pull together the parish mission or vision statements, pastoral planning document(s), or short- or long-term strategic plans. He might ask the parish staff, parish council, finance council, or parishioners whether these documents have been developed. If they exist, what process was used to develop them? Have they been in place for a long time, or are they relatively recent (within the last two or three years)?

Archdiocesan/Diocesan Policies

Archdioceses/dioceses have financial plans and policies that Fr. Dave will want to review. These policies will include recommendations or mandates to ensure that he is following guidelines and mandates, and is prepared to deliver to the archdiocese/diocese required information. This information can be extremely helpful because many outline specific steps to complete as well as the requirements for preparing financial reports.

> The Catholic Diocese of Trenton (New Jersey) publishes an extensive parish financial management guide to assist parishes on budgeting and financial management. Often these documents can be found online.

Current Year Budget and Actuals

Fr. Dave should collect the most recent budget as well as the actual income and expenses for the current twelve-month period. This data will be crucial as he develops budget estimates for income and expenses. The parish financial software can be used to gather this information.

Prior Year Actuals

Fr. Dave will find it helpful to collect the actual income and expense information from the previous two or three years by budget category. This will enable him to forecast income and expenses.

Budget Formulation Methods

Budget development is like building a house. In order to complete the house, it needs to have the foundation laid, the walls raised, and the roof built before starting on the interior. Sometimes we seem to construct the roof before the foundation! Like building a house, the architecture plans are established when you develop your budget process. The foundation and walls may already be established (archdiocesan/diocesan policies), and you may already be aware of what it will take to bring the house up to code (canon law). Now you are ready for budget formulation, which is the process of doing the detailed work of putting in new floors, painting walls, and buying appliances.

There are multiple methods to develop a budget, and given that we are now going to forecast resources that we expect to come in (income) and spend (expenses), there is always going to be a level of uncertainty, no matter how we approach the topic.

To determine the methods we will use to develop estimates, it is important to begin with understanding, at a high level, three overall approaches to budgeting: top-down, bottom-up or zero-based budgeting, and incremental budget formulation.

Figure 4-1
Budget formulation methods

Whether budgets are developed from one method or a hybrid, there are inherent advantages and disadvantages of each method, and understanding these approaches can help you determine how you might put these in place at your parish.

Top-Down Budgeting

A **top-down** approach to budgeting is when resources are allocated at a high level and the details are then worked out based on this amount of funding. To use a simple example, think about your salary. Each month, your employer gives you a salary but does not dictate how you spend that money. Unless a pay raise is on the horizon, you know how much money you have available to spend and you work out your budget based on that amount of money. The same method can be applied to parish budgeting. In certain organizations, a leader will establish how much money will be allocated for a given project and then the budget is created from that level of funding. On the other hand, maybe you receive a donation from a benefactor and you are going to budget those resources using this method.

The advantage of top-down budgeting is that the method is relatively simple. It does not necessarily require labor-intensive cost estimating because the overall amount of money that will be budgeted is established. Using this method, money is then allocated to categories of spending. One disadvantage to top-down budgeting is that you might be forcing or formfitting various cost elements to meet your target.

In an initial meeting with Fr. Dave, Michele (director of faith formation) mentioned a new initiative to create an adult faith formation speaker series. Fr. Dave told Michele, "I see that we have allocated money in previous years for adult faith formation. If we were to allocate eight thousand dollars for this purpose, what would you propose?" Using the top-down budgeting method, Michele divides the funding into three categories: speaker stipends, food and beverage, and publicity. Table 4-1 displays how Michele divided the budget.

Table 4-1
St. Michael's faith formation program
Top-down budget example

Allocated Budget	$8,000
Speaker Stipends	-$4,000
Food and Beverage	-$3,500
Publicity	-$500

Top-down budgeting works very well when you know the amount of money you are willing to allocate or you have a set amount of funding given by an external source. The key is to involve and empower others who will help you manage the budget so buy-in is established early in this process. In general, if the top-down method is applied to budget formulation, it is important that those responsible for managing the budget propose and justify enhancements or reductions for the budget they have been allocated. A simple method would involve asking Michele to detail how she plans to spend the money *and* allow her an opportunity to propose changes based on her estimates if the money Fr. Dave proposed is too much or too little.

In this example, involving Michele in determining a plan for the money to be spent is a best practice. A disadvantage to this budgeting method is that she may feel as if this budget has been forced upon her. As we will learn in upcoming chapters, this may also cause challenges related to future budget execution and control. If a top-down method is applied to an organization without the collaboration of those responsible for managing the budget, ownership by Michele for meeting spending goals may not be as strong. For example, if, at the midyear budget review meeting, there's been too much spending for event publicity and Michele is asked about this she may say, "Well, I was given a budget and I made it work." Without collaboration, a layer of accountability is taken away.

You may now be saying, "Ok, but staff will always seek more resources, right?" Again, this is where collaboration is so critical in budget matters. When staff members are empowered and know that they have input into budget formulation, it is much less likely that unreasonable requests are proposed. Budgets that are developed secretly or through closed-door methods serve no one well and actually diminish staff morale. Top-down budgeting works well when those who will manage the budget are involved in the process.

Bottom-Up or Zero-Based Budgeting

The second formulation method is a **bottom-up** approach, sometimes referred to as **zero-based budgeting**. This method involves building a budget from the lowest income/expense elements and then rolling them up into the total budget request. From zero, each cost element is developed and justified.

Therefore when the budget is complete, the program manager has a thorough understanding of the budget under their management.

The advantage of this method is that each cost element is scrutinized and justified in order to develop the budget. The challenge to this type of method is that it can be time consuming due to the comprehensive nature of building from zero up. Therefore, the leader might consider using this method for one department at a time or taking a bottom-up approach every other year so that the process is not overwhelming for those involved in building the budget. When a budget has been developed using the bottom-up approach method, the insight into a program/department is typically very good.

Another advantage to this method is that the detailed analysis provides a level of granularity not necessarily achieved by top-down budgeting. With top-down budgeting, the dollars are broken out from a broader perspective, whereas the bottom-up method creates a more precise estimate of program costs. Let's review an example at St. Michael's.

St. Michael's—Bottom-Up Budgeting

When using a bottom-up approach to building the budget for the speaker series, Michele will start from the lowest level of spending and develop estimates per category that roll up to the larger budget request. Below is a sample for how this might look when preparing the budget for the speaker series. Table 4-2 displays how Michele divided the budget using a bottom-up approach.

Table 4-2
St. Michael's faith formation program
Bottom-up budget example

Speaker Stipends	# of speakers *multiplied* $ stipend per speaker
	Speaker stipends = 6 speakers x $600 stipend
	= **$ 3,600**
Food and Beverage for Participants	# of events *multiplied* $ food estimate per event
	6 events x $500
	= **$ 3,000**
Publicity	$.05 per copy of advertisement *multiplied* (# of copies *multiplied* # of events)
	($.05 per copy) x (750 of copies x 6 events)
	= **$ 225**
Faith Formation Budget Request	+ $ 3,600 speaker stipends
	+ $ 3,000 food and beverage
	+ $ 225 publicity
	= **$ 6,825**

Recognizing that the bottom-up approach may take more time than other methods, address the limitations of this approach up front with clear guidance. Be sure to state that even though the level of time and energy required can be taxing, it is worth the effort because the level of details that are generated assist the team in making better and more informed decisions. For example, if later in the year money becomes available or budget reductions are needed, the bottom-up approach provides a level of granularity to allow more precise decisions on where to enhance or cut funding. Therefore, because this budget has been developed with an attention to details, the impact is more readily known.

Incremental Budgeting

Incremental budgeting is the simplest technique to implement and is common across many parishes as budgets are developed. Incremental budgeting involves determining a percentage increase or decrease for budget line items and then multiplying this percentage across categories. This technique has the distinct advantage of not involving complex forecasting or cost estimating and can be applied across a wide range of data.

St. Michael's—Incremental Budgeting

Instead of using the other methods, Fr. Dave and Michele determine that they will use an incremental budgeting method and apply a 3 percent increase across all categories related to the faith formation at St. Michael's. There are three primary programs with specific budget line items related to faith formation. With this method, Michele will take the prior year budget and multiply the 3 percent increase across the categories and a new baseline would be established for these programs.

Table 4-3
St. Michael's faith formation program
Incremental budget example

		A	B	C	D
Line Item	Category	Prior Year Budget	% Change	Amount Change (A x B)	FY 20XX Proposed (A + C)
2501	RCIA	$12,000	3%	$360	$12,360
2502	Religious Education	$10,000	3%	$300	$10,300
2503	Adult Faith Formation	$10,000	3%	$300	$10,300
2504	Young Adults	$2,000	3%	$60	$2,060
2506	Vacation Bible School	$5,000	3%	$150	$5,150
	Faith Formation Total	**$39,000**		**$1,170**	**$40,170**

As you can see in table 4-3, the new budget for the faith formation program line items is $40,170, a 3 percent increase from the prior year's budget.

Now you may be asking yourself, "Ok, that seems simple enough, but how do you determine the percentage increase/decrease?"

You may not believe it, but some organizations simply guesstimate the percentage. This is when budgeting becomes more of an art than a science. For example, the parish may believe that they will receive an increase in funding. However, the reality is that the opposite situation is more common.

For example, let's say that the pastoral team has discussed that there will be a decline in collections based on the year-over-year declines in the prior year periods. Therefore, the team decided to reduce the budget. If we are looking for a balanced budget, this will mean that the budget will need to be decreased across a number of spending categories. The pastoral team may estimate that there will be a reduction of approximately 1 percent in income for the upcoming year. The simplest approach would be to take the 1 percent and reduce all categories by this percentage.

This may be OK if your income and expenses are very stable year in and year out; however, to become more accurate, the recommendation would be to add some precision to the incremental budget process. This is when a combination of budget methods may be in order to get the most accurate and efficient budget. When a straight percentage is applied to all categories indiscriminately, you lose a layer of analysis that would allow you to see some categories that may not need as much money as previous years or other categories that have been underfunded. After this review, you may find that the incremental approach works for a number of categories but that the bottom-up budget method is more effective for those budget line items that are sensitive or more inconsistent year to year.

Chapter Summary

The budget formulation phase should begin by gathering the parish and vision statements, reviewing any strategic or pastoral planning documentation, and continuing to dialogue with staff and parishioners on how they see the parish presently and into the future. Be sure to collect all applicable archdiocesan/diocesan financial policies and procedures, and export (from your financial software) income and expense data for the current and past year. In your arsenal of tools, you now have three budget formulation frameworks available to you for building the various elements of the budget. Whether you decide to use a top-down, bottom-up, incremental, or hybrid approach to budgeting, these methods are part of your tool kit for getting started with building any aspect of a budget.

Next in chapter 5, we jump into the nuts and bolts of building a budget. We'll discuss forecasting income, estimating expenses, and creating a budget that is not only comprehensive but also practical.

Chapter 5

Budget Formulation Part II

Nuts and Bolts of Building a Budget

Chapter 5 Preview

In this chapter, we help Fr. Dave to do the following:

- Create a cash flow budget
- Learn forecasting techniques
- Understand the steps in estimating parish income and expenses
  - Step 1: Collect data
  - Step 2: Prioritize time
  - Step 3: Forecast and document assumptions
  - Step 4: Present and finalize
- Discuss best practices in presenting the budget to stakeholders

St. Michael's Parish—Parish Income and Expenses

Fr. Dave has never estimated, projected, or even submitted a budget. Where does he begin? As we will discover in this chapter, we have a number of techniques that Fr. Dave will use to plan and estimate income and expenses. Mary has presented him with a proposed budget for next year, but it still seems overwhelming.

Fr. Dave has made good progress in learning budget fundamentals, understanding how the budget lifecycle works, and implementing budget methods (top-down, bottom-up, incremental) to allocate resources. Now he is ready to roll up his sleeves and go deep into forecasting income and expenses and creating a master budget to most effectively manage parish finances.

Table 5-1
St. Michael's annual budget

Line Item	Category	Amount
Income		
1000	Collections	$707,000
1100	Donations	$16,500
1200	Programs	$7,500
1300	Other Income	$14,000
	Total Income	**$745,000**
Expenses		
2000	Personnel/Salary	$182,000
2100	Personnel/Other	$82,121
2200	Diocesan Assessment	$70,700
2300	Administrative/Office	$89,145
2400	Liturgical/Sacramental	$45,500
2500	Programs	$58,000
2600	Plant/Facilities	$115,700
	Total Expenses	**$643,166**
	Surplus/Deficit	**$101,834**

Parish Income and Expenses

As displayed in table 5-1, the annual budget provides Fr. Dave with the ability to quickly review the annual amounts that the parish has allocated for income (collections, donations, etc.) and expenses (salary and benefits, administrative/office, programs, etc.) categories. Based on the annual budget summary, church expenses subtracted from church income will deliver a surplus of money for St. Michael's. Although the budget displayed in this format can provide a quick overview of the parish budget, it is missing critical and necessary information.

Reflection Question:
What are some of the elements that we have already discussed that are missing in this budget representation?

Here are some possible responses to the reflection question above:

1. What assumptions have been built into the budget?

2. Are any income or expenses categories variable month by month or are the amounts the same throughout the year? For example, are there periods of time during the year that more money is spent on a specific category? Are any of the plant/facilities costs variable based on the month of the year?

3. For salaries and benefits, how are salaries broken out by individual?

4. Does the parish have any investments, endowments, or other savings accounts?

In order to address these responses, we first need to structure the budget in a format that makes sense to help the parish manage the finances most effectively. The cash flow budget is an excellent way to begin breaking the budget down into manageable parts.

Creating a Cash Flow Budget

The budget that Mary provided Fr. Dave gave him the annual amounts of money that have been budgeted, but it doesn't give a good idea of how the money will flow throughout the year. As the name implies, the **cash flow budget** provides estimates for the amount of money that the parish expects to receive and expects to spend for a given time period. Typically, the cash flow budget is broken down by months, but this form of the budget can be further broken down by weeks or even by days.

The reason the cash flow budget is an effective mode for developing the budget is that parishes typically do not receive or spend the same amounts of money each month. Therefore, the cash flow budget can provide an adequate level of detail for effective management of parish finances.

Collections fluctuate as the church seasons change, and therefore total monthly income will also change. For example, in December, the parish expects to receive the Christmas collection. With the cash flow budget, the parish will know how much cash will be available to pay actual expenses. If your parish income and expenses are consistent across the different months, this is even easier, but we still recommend that you begin by creating the budget by month and then, if necessary, in the future you can go into more detail.

Our ultimate goal in building any budget is to build the foundation for a balanced budget. A **balanced budget** is achieved when income minus expenses are equal or greater than zero. If money remains after all expenses have been paid for in a given month, we can say that the budget has achieved a **surplus**. The surplus can then be used either for other months when the cash is limited or it can be placed into savings. If expenses are more than income, the budget contains a **deficit**.

Before moving on though, it is important to clarify surpluses and deficits. Many church managers get very concerned when they see a budget has some months with "deficits" and others with "surpluses." However, you must be cautious in recognizing when deficits are problematic and when deficits are acceptable. The good news is that the cash flow budget actually addresses these concerns. The cash flow budget helps to identify the ebbs and flows of the budget, allowing you to take action early in the budget process so that you set yourself up for success.

Below are some key conditions when surpluses and deficits are not necessarily problematic.

1. Each month you have more than enough cash available to pay all expenses.

2. When surpluses are available, you employ a "savings strategy."

3. At the end of the fiscal year, the parish budget is balanced with a goal to have surplus funds.

You are not alone if you have been unable to save money or you have tapped savings to meet operating expenses. However, this is not a sustainable long-term solution. Our goal is to help you get out of that pattern and get your parish on track by creating reserves.

Now that we have established that we want to build a cash flow budget, let's take all of the concepts and go in depth on how to create it!

Introduction to Basic Forecasting

Often, when the word **forecasting** comes up, most people believe that unless you have a background in statistics, you must rely on others to undertake this task. We believe that forecasting can be accessible to anyone willing to learn some basic techniques (see references at the conclusion of this chapter).

Webster's Dictionary defines forecasting as "calculating or predicting (some future event or condition) usually as a result of study and analysis of available pertinent data." Whenever you predict anything, it involves your best estimate, or *guesstimate*, of what will happen. The good news is that you usually have some level of information or data that can help guide you, but that's not all. You also have people around you who have experience and can provide their insights on what they believe will happen. Human judgment plays a significant role in forecasting. As pointed out by many of the leading forecasters, "the most effective forecaster is able to formulate a skillful mix of quantitative forecasting techniques and good judgment and to avoid the extremes of total reliance on either."[1] Therefore, relying on historical data and human judgment can provide the foundation for your income and expense forecasts.

Step 1: Collect Data

History is a great predictor of the future and therefore you can use the most current data available to help in this process. There is a caveat to collecting historical data. Data must always be relevant for the greatest accuracy in forecasting. Defining which types of data are most "relevant" for your parish can be more of an art than science, but with forecasting, practicing the strategies outlined (that follow) will help.

If history is a good predictor of the future, then start with information that is actually known. In budgeting, use the "actuals" for a given category and period. With actuals, the information is not theoretical. *Actuals* are the amounts of money received or spent. Collect the actuals from the current year for the same time period you are budgeting. For example, what is the actual amount of income received for the prior twelve months? This data will give you a nice starting point to determine where to focus.

Why is it so important to have historical data? With data from the past, you can attempt to identify patterns (trends), make assumptions about the future, and then test the model using prior-year data to make the best prediction.

St. Michael's Example—Collect Data

Fr. Dave will collect actual data from the prior year for St. Michael's. Table 5-2 displays the totals for the actual income received. As you can see, the parish received $707,000 from a variety of collections, $16,500 from donations, $7,500 from programs, and $14,000 from other income for a total of $745,000.

Table 5-2
St. Michael's operating income

Line Item	Category	Amount
1000 Collections		
1001	Sunday Collections	$620,000
1002	Holy Day Collections	$75,000
1003	Parish Needs Collections	$12,000

Table 5-2 continued on next page

1. John E. Henke and Arthur G. Reitsch, *Business Forecasting*, 6th ed. (Upper Saddle River, NJ: Prentice Hall, 1998), 2.

Table 5-2 continued

	Total Collections	$707,000
Line Item	**Category**	**Amount**
1100 Donations		
1101	Stole (Baptism, Weddings, Funerals)	$10,000
1102	Flowers	$2,500
1103	Candles	$4,000
	Total Donations	**$16,500**
1200 Programs		
1201	Religious Education	$5,000
1202	Adult Education	$1,000
1203	Parish Picnic	$1,500
	Total Program Fees	**$7,500**
1300 Other Income		
1301	Church Bulletin Advertising/Misc.	$10,000
1302	Sales of Literature/Goods	$1,500
1303	Interest and Dividends	$2,500
	Total Other Income	**$14,000**
	TOTAL INCOME	**$745,000**

There is no doubt that parish managers are busy people, so the next step in the process is to take the data that has been collected and focus your time. Focusing on the "right" areas of the budget means prioritizing your time so that you spend the greatest amount of effort on those areas that will provide the most significant benefits. A nice tool to deploy during this phase of the process is to calculate the *Budget Category Impact Percentage.*

Step 2: Prioritize Time

If time is money, the **Budget Category Impact Percentage (BCIP)** calculation is a simple formula that can assist you to quickly assess the relative size of a specific budget category as compared to the total spending for the overall income or expense category. If you calculate which categories have the greatest impact on the budget, you can spend the majority of your time focusing on those areas.

St. Michael's Example—Calculating the BCIP for Income

To calculate the BCIP, Fr. Dave will take each income category's annual amount and divide the amount by the total church income. Once completed, this information will provide him with a percentage of the category impact on total church income. Using a spreadsheet or other mode to make calculations, he can make the calculations using equation 5-1.

Equation 5-1

Budget Category Impact Percentage Calculation (BCIP): income category annual amount ÷ total church income

    Examples

1. (1001) Sunday Collections	=	Sunday Collection ÷ Total Church Income
	=	$620,000 ÷ $745,000
	=	83.2%
2. (1002) Holy Day Collections	=	Holy Day Collections ÷ Total Church Income
	=	$75,000 ÷ $745,000
	=	10.1%
3. (1003) Parish Needs Collections	=	Parish Needs Collections ÷ Total Church Income
	=	$12,000 ÷ $745,000
	=	1.6%

Next, Fr. Dave can continue calculating the BCIP for all income categories. After the calculations have been completed, the information is consolidated and displayed in table 5-3.

Table 5-3
St. Michael's operating income
Budget Category Income Percentage

Line Item	Category	Amount	As % of Total Income
1000 Collections			
1001	Sunday Collections	$620,000	83.2%
1002	Holy Day Collections	$75,000	10.1%
1003	Parish Needs Collections	$12,000	1.6%
	Total Collections	**$707,000**	**94.9%**
1100 Donations			
1101	Stole (Baptism, Weddings, Funerals)	$10,000	1.3%
1102	Flowers	$2,500	0.3%
1103	Candles	$4,000	0.5%
	Total Donations	**$16,500**	**2.2%**
1200 Programs			
1201	Religious Education	$5,000	0.7%
1202	Adult Education	$1,000	0.1%
1203	Parish Picnic	$1,500	0.2%
	Total Program Fees	**$7,500**	**1.0%**
1300 Other Income			
1301	Church Bulletin Advertising/Misc.	$10,000	1.3%
1302	Sales of Literature/Goods	$1,500	0.2%
1303	Interest and Dividends	$2,500	0.3%
	Total Other Income	**$14,000**	**1.9%**
	TOTAL INCOME	**$745,000**	**100%**

The principle for using BCIP is to allow Fr. Dave and his team to focus on the income categories with the greatest impact on the budget. For St. Michael's, it is clear what drives income—Sunday collections account for 83.2 percent of the total income. With more than three-quarters of income derived from Sunday collections, prioritizing this budget category will be a good place to start. Armed with this information, Fr. Dave can now develop a forecast for collections.

Step 3: Forecast and Document Assumptions

With the list of prioritized categories, the budget methods we discussed in chapter 4 (top-down, bottom-up, incremental) will help you develop the budget.

When preparing a budget, you will use assumptions to guide the direction of various components of your budget. A best practice in budget formulation involves writing these assumptions down so you can return to them in the future and review their adequacy or relevancy to what actually occurred. When analyzing budget data, whether the assumptions are written or not, the key is to think through the assumptions you developed so you can either validate or modify them based on changing circumstances.

Be sure to keep a list of budget assumptions as you develop these forecasts.

Parish Income

A significant driver of parish income is Sunday, holy day, and special collections. There are also other categories of income that include donations for specific purposes (stole fees, flowers, candles) as well as fees related to parish programs. Other income may come in the form of money paid for advertising in the bulletin, sale of literature and books, and interest and dividends. The lists of income categories across parishes varies, but when getting started with parish income, focus on the category that drives the greatest percentage of total income—collections.

Forecasting Church Collections

If you are anxious about forecasting collections, you are not alone. It can be a challenging and sensitive area for parish life. Why? It has become stressful because collections (Sundays, holy days, etc.) depend upon a factor that is increasingly more challenging to predict—church attendance! Unfortunately, in North America, church attendance has been declining. According to a study by the *Center for Applied Research in the Apostolate*, the average church attendance at parishes has declined from 35 percent in 1995 to 24 percent in 2014.

Whether parishioner attendance is up or down, using the data you currently have available, along with your judgment, you can deploy some tools.

Where to begin? Start with actuals from the current year, and gather data from the previous year or even two or three years. You can pull this data from your parish financial software. It will also be helpful to have the current parish statistics:

- Number of registered parishioner households
- Number of sacraments administered
- Average weekly attendance
- Data on holy day and special collections

If all of this information is not available, do not worry. The number of registered parishioners can be a good place to start.

St. Michael's Example—Collecting Data

Fr. Dave knows that there are thirteen hundred registered families in the parish. According to the data, $620,000 was collected over the past twelve months. Taking this, he can quickly calculate the average annual Sunday collection per registered family.

Equation 5-2
Average Annual Sunday Collection per Registered Family

Average Annual Collection per Family = Total Sunday Offerings (Annual) ÷
                                          # Registered Households
                                       = $620,000 ÷ 1,300
                                       = $477

According to the calculations above, on average, St. Michael's receives $477—note that numbers are rounded to the nearest dollar—per year, per registered family for Sunday collections. Therefore, registered families are contributing approximately $40 per month. This may or may not seem like a large sum of money, but remember, this calculation is one data point for Fr. Dave to consider as he seeks to forecast Sunday collections.

Conducting Sensitivity Analysis

The principle of using sensitivity analysis is to help you plan for the variety of outcomes that can occur given any change in circumstances. You might ask, "What happens if the number of registered families decreases at our parish—will we then overestimate income?" This is where sensitivity analysis can help. The analysis helps answer the question, "What happens if...?" Therefore, you have a tool at your disposal to mitigate a wide variety of outcomes or changes in circumstances.

Let's use sensitivity analysis to calculate what happens if the number of registered families increases or decreases at the parish. You can multiply the various changes in the number of registered families by the result of equation 5-2 above. The results are found in table 5-4, and you can see the various impacts on annual (and monthly) collections.

Table 5-4
Sensitivity analysis of registered families (decreases/increases)
St. Michael's Sunday collections

	Decreases		Current	Increases	
% Change	**-6%**	**-3%**	**No Change**	**3%**	**6%**
# Registered Families	1,222	1,261	**1,300**	1,339	1,378
Average **Annual** Sunday Collection per Family	$477	$477	**$477**	$477	$477
Projected Sunday Collection (Annual)	**$582,894**	**$601,497**	**$619,996**	**$638,703**	**$657,306**
Projected Sunday Collection (Monthly)	**$48,575**	**$50,125**	**$51,666**	**$53,225**	**$54,776**

After a sensitivity analysis is performed, you now have another data element that you may wish to use when developing your collections forecast.

Average Sunday Collection per Mass Attendee

Let's say you are skeptical of this method because you do not believe that the number of registered households is a good indicator for determining annual collections. For example, what if a parish has a high number of registered households, but the actual number of Mass attendees is very low. How could you adjust this method for other data you may have?

Here is a simple strategy: Determine the average number of weekly Mass attendees by gathering parish volunteers to act as "attendee counters." The more data you are able to collect on the average number of attendees, the more accurate your forecast may become. The only way to see if this method works for your parish is to test it.

St. Michael's Example

A group of St. Michael's parishioners signs up and counts attendees at the weekend liturgies for two months. Table 5-5 displays the data collected along with the weekly collection amounts.

Table 5-5
Summary of Sunday Mass attendees and weekly collections

Month	Week	Number of Attendees	Weekly Collection
Month 1	Week 1	1,814	$12,916
	Week 2	1,776	$12,513
	Week 3	1,890	$13,250
	Week 4	1,924	$15,201
	Month 1 Total	**7,404**	**$53,880**
Month 2	Week 5	1,901	$15,140
	Week 6	1,865	$13,110
	Week 7	1,800	$12,500
	Week 8	1,898	$13,350
	Month 2 Total	**7,464**	**$54,100**
Two-Monthly Average		**7,434**	**$53,990**

Now that the data is compiled, we can calculate the average collection amount per attendee by dividing the weekly collection by the number of attendees.

Equation 5-3
Calculating the Average Weekly Collection per Attendee: total weekly collection ÷ # attendees

Week 1	=	$12,916 ÷ 1,814 attendees
	=	**$7.12 per attendee**
Week 2	=	$12,513 ÷ 1,776 attendees
	=	**$7.05 per attendee**
Week 3	=	$13,250 ÷ 1,890 attendees
	=	**$7.01 per attendee**
Week 4	=	15,201 ÷ 1,924 attendees
	=	**$7.90 per attendee**

Table 5-6
Average weekly collection per attendee summary

Month	Week	Number of Attendees	Weekly Collection	Average Weekly Collection Amount per Attendee
Month 1	Week 1	1,814	$12,916	$7.12
	Week 2	1,776	$12,513	$7.05
	Week 3	1,890	$13,250	$7.01
	Week 4	1,924	$15,201	$7.90
	Month 1 Total	**7,404**	**$53,880**	**$7.28**
Month 2	Week 5	1,901	$15,140	$7.96
	Week 6	1,865	$13,110	$7.03
	Week 7	1,800	$12,500	$6.94
	Week 8	1,898	$13,350	$7.03
	Month 2 Total	**7,464**	**$54,100**	
Monthly Average		**7,434**	**$53,990**	**$7.26**

As shown by table 5-6, the average collection amount per attendee is $7.26. You will also see that for the two-month period, the monthly collection averages $53,990. With this information available, you can now conduct a sensitivity analysis to determine the impact on monthly collections as attendance at liturgy increases or decreases.

Table 5-7
Sensitivity analysis of attendees and collections

	Decreases		Current	Increases	
% Change	**-10%**	**-5%**	**No Change**	**5%**	**10%**
Average # of Weekly Attendees	6,691	7,062	**7,434**	7,806	8,177
Average Weekly Collection per Attendee	$7.26	$7.26	$7.26	$7.26	$7.26
Projected Sunday Collection (Monthly)	**$48,574**	**$51,272**	**$53,971**	**$56,669**	**$59,368**
Projected Sunday Collection (Annual)	**$582,885**	**$615,268**	**$647,650**	**$680,033**	**$712,415**

Table 5-7 provides us an additional data point in projecting income. If you calculate the difference between the two methods, you see a variation in the annual collection of $27,654 and $2,305 in the monthly projection. As displayed in table 5-8, the difference between the two methods is only 4 percent.

Table 5-8

Comparison of registered family and attendee impact on collections

	Registered Family Method	Attendee Method	Variance	% Difference
Projected Collection (Monthly)	$51,666	$53,971	($2,305)	-4%
Projected Collection (Annual)	$619,996	$647,650	($27,654)	-4%

When building the forecast for the next year, you might even consider averaging the two projected amounts [($619,996 + $647,650) ÷ 2] and create a forecast for an annual collection amount of $633,823.

How do you determine which method to use? The answer depends upon your best judgment based on your experience. If you are unsure, the only way to validate your method is to test it. Pick one method and after a few months, you will have collected actual data. You'll then be able to compare and contrast the forecast to the actual data.

When forecasting other income categories, the same principles apply. Collect actual data per spending category (for example, find out the amount of income the parish received for stole fees). Next, determine if there are any changes that would be necessary to adjust the budget line item. Create a list of any assumptions you have made and using one of the methods we described in chapter 4 (top-down, bottom-up, incremental), forecast the income category.

Parish Expenses

Now that we have reviewed parish income, let's turn to parish expenses. First, like parish income, we will want to calculate the Budget Category Impact Percentage (BCIP). After reviewing the data, table 5-9 shows the BCIP for parish expenses. Like most parishes, the driving expenses of this parish include expenses related to salary and benefits, the physical plant, and administrative expenses.

Table 5-9
Budget Category Income Percentage
Parish expenses

Line Item	Category	Amount	As % of Total Expenses
2000 Personnel/Salaries			
2001	Pastor	$33,500	5.2%
2002	Business Manager	$21,000	3.3%
2003	Secretary	$31,000	4.8%
2004	Music	$33,000	5.1%
2005	Faith Formation	$35,000	5.4%
2006	Maintenance Manager	$28,500	4.4%
	Total Personnel/Salary	**$182,000**	**28.3%**

Table 5-9 continued on pages 42–43

Table 5-9 continued

Line Item	Category	Amount	As % of Total Expenses
2100 Personnel/Other			
2101	Lay Medical Insurance	$20,000	3.1%
2102	Clergy Insurance	$31,000	4.8%
2103	Employer Social Security	$11,284	1.8%
2104	Employer Medicare	$2,730	0.4%
2105	Lay Employee Retirement	$4,455	0.7%
2106	Workers' Comp. and Disability	$3,640	0.6%
2107	Unemployment Insurance	$2,912	0.5%
2108	ADP Payroll Expense	$450	0.1%
2109	Retreats and Workshops	$2,000	0.3%
2110	Lay Training	$2,000	0.3%
2111	Associations/Memberships	$650	0.1%
2112	Gifts and Bonuses	$1,000	0.2%
	Total Personnel/Other	**$82,121**	**12.8%**
2200 Diocesan/Other			
2201	Diocesan Assessment	$70,700	11.0%
	Total Diocesan	**$70,700**	**11.0%**
2300 Administrative/Office			
2301	Supplies and Equipment	$4,500	0.7%
2302	Postage	$3,000	0.5%
2303	Printing and Copying	$10,000	1.6%
2304	Offertory Envelopes	$10,345	1.6%
2305	Advertising	$1,600	0.2%
2306	Audit and Legal Services	$1,500	0.2%
2307	Security System	$1,300	0.2%
2308	Internet	$2,400	0.4%
2309	Office Phones	$5,500	0.9%
2310	Cell Phones	$3,000	0.5%
2311	Website Support and Development	$3,000	0.5%
2312	Automobile and Travel	$10,000	1.6%
2313	Priest Reimbursement	$4,500	0.7%
2314	Parish Meals and Hosting	$3,500	0.5%
2315	Interest and Bank Charges	$1,000	0.2%
2316	Criminal Background Checks	$2,000	0.3%
2317	Contracted Services	$10,000	1.6%
2318	Extra Clergy Assistance	$5,000	0.8%
2319	Fundraising	$3,000	0.5%
2320	Parish Hall Supplies	$4,000	0.6%
	Total Administrative/Office	**$89,145**	**13.9%**

Table 5-9 continued on next page

Table 5-9 continued

Line Item	Category	Amount	As % of Total Expenses
2400 Liturgical/Sacramental			
2401	Liturgical Supplies	$10,000	1.6%
2402	Flowers	$3,500	0.5%
2403	Vestments	$1,000	0.2%
2404	Liturgical Seasons	$3,000	0.5%
2405	Sacramental Supplies (Baptism, Confirmation, etc.)	$3,000	0.5%
2406	Music Program	$20,000	3.1%
2407	Music Publications	$5,000	0.8%
	Total Liturgical/Sacramental	**$45,500**	**7.1%**
2500 Programs			
2501	RCIA	$12,000	1.9%
2502	Religious Education	$10,000	1.6%
2503	Adult Faith Formation	$10,000	1.6%
2504	Young Adults	$2,000	0.3%
2505	Vacation Bible School	$5,000	0.8%
2506	Parish Events	$5,000	0.8%
2507	Parish Picnic	$3,000	0.5%
2508	Evangelization	$8,000	1.2%
2509	Social Justice Programs	$1,500	0.2%
2510	Councils and Committees	$1,500	0.2%
	Total Programs	**$58,000**	**9.0%**
2600 Plant/Facilities			
2601	Water and Sewer	$3,900	0.6%
2602	Electric	$13,000	2.0%
2603	Building Supplies	$5,000	0.8%
2604	Regular Building Maintenance	$15,000	2.3%
2605	Building Repairs	$15,000	2.3%
2606	Pest and Termite Control	$2,500	0.4%
2607	Grounds Maintenance	$15,000	2.3%
2608	Equipment Repair	$10,000	1.6%
2609	Real Estate Taxes	$1,300	0.2%
2610	Property and Liability Insurance	$35,000	5.4%
	Total Plant/Facilities	**$115,700**	**18.0%**
	TOTAL EXPENSES	**$643,166**	**100%**

Given the level of simplicity of today's spreadsheet and other financial software, Fr. Dave could also display this information in a graphic. For visual people, graphics can be extremely helpful to identify patterns, trends, and standout items. Figure 5-1 displays the information in a doughnut chart.

Figure 5-1
Parish expenses as a percentage of total expenses

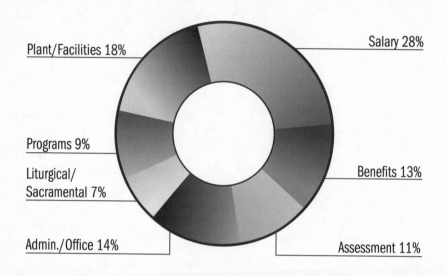

Plant/Facilities 18%

Salary 28%

Programs 9%

Liturgical/
Sacramental 7%

Benefits 13%

Admin./Office 14%

Assessment 11%

Fixed and Variable Costs

Now that we have prioritized the expenses, review the list and break the list down by cost type—fixed or variable costs. **Fixed costs** are expenses that do not change as volume increases or decreases for services offered. Alternatively, **variable costs** are those expenses that directly change as a result of the variation in the volume of services delivered.

What are the services offered when it comes to parish life? Examples include administering the sacraments, offering education programs, distributing food to the less fortunate, ministering to the needy, and the list goes on and on. What programs and services does your parish offer? Then, for each line item, determine to what extent the expenses are directly or indirectly related to the "volume."

Often, fixed costs are recurring expenses that do not vary month to month. Examples include mortgager or lease payments, salary and benefits, and debt repayment. Variable costs, on the other hand, are those expenses that may fluctuate month to month. Utilities and grounds maintenance are good examples of variable costs, due to seasonality. Additionally, liturgical and sacramental expenses may vary with the volume of people that attend liturgies. As the number of people in the pews increases or decreases, the parish will adjust the amount of sacramental supplies that are purchased. Breaking down costs into fixed and variable is especially important for parish school and education programs. The costs related to these programs typically depend upon the number of enrolled students. Therefore, understanding the effect that changes have on the budget will be important.

When forecasting expenses, the place to start is to review the amount of money (actuals) paid in the last twelve months. Next, determine whether the amounts of money paid have varied month to month and even year to year. If the amount has varied, investigate further to seek understanding on why. If you find yourself with limited time, use the BCIP exercise (table 5-3 and table 5-9) to focus your analysis.

Let's review some of the expense categories in St. Michael's budget.

Personnel: Salary and Benefits

A major category of spending related to any organization is salary and benefits. This makes complete sense because people are the driving force behind any organization. In 2005, the United States Conference of Catholic Bishops (USCCB) published a landmark document, *Co-workers in the Vineyard of the Lord*, which was influential in defining the roles, responsibilities, and identity of the lay ecclesial minister in the Catholic Church today. As part of this document, the Bishops' Conference developed a framework in order to assist dioceses across the country with developing and guiding programs for lay ecclesial ministers. One of the key aspects of this program includes a call for fair and equitable compensation for all church workers.

Co-workers in the Vineyard of the Lord

While not all those working for the Church are paid, all deserve recognition and affirmation of their contribution to its mission. Those lay ecclesial ministers serving in paid positions need fair compensation for their work. The Church has a long history of speaking about the dignity of work and the proper recognition of people's service. In a comprehensive personnel system, this area includes salary plans that may establish ranges through which individuals may progress, as well as benefit plans (e.g., health insurance, family leave, child care assistance, funding for ongoing education). These issues can be particularly challenging when resources are limited. Compensation packages vary from one geographic region to another depending on the finances of each diocese and the cost of living in a given area.

—United States Conference of Catholic Bishops (USCCB),
Co-workers in the Vineyard of the Lord
(Washington, DC: USCCB, 2005), 63.

Personnel policies and procedures vary by location. However, there are a number of resources available to assist you with learning more about all aspects of human resources management, including staff recruitment, compensation, performance evaluation, and retention of staff. As it relates to budgeting salaries, consider these questions:

- Are any staff eligible for a raise in the upcoming year, and at what percentage?
- During what month would raise(s) occur?
- Does the parish plan to hire any new staff? If so, what is the expected month that the employee will be hired? What is the projected compensation?

By answering these brief questions, you can then adjust staff salary to reflect anticipated changes in the budget forecast. Let's say you want to calculate the impact of a specific percentage change on staff salaries. Create a quick worksheet like the one displayed in table 5-10 to summarize your data. Use the incremental budget method and quickly calculate the impact on the personnel budget.

Table 5-10
Staff salary adjustment worksheet

		A	B	C	D
Line Item	**Category**	**Annual Salary**	**% Change**	**Amount Change**	**Adjusted Annual Salary**
Enter code	Enter title A	Enter salary	Enter % adjustment	Calculate **A x B**	Calculate **A + C**
Enter code	Enter title B	Enter salary	Enter % adjustment	Calculate **A x B**	Calculate **A + C**

Once salaries have been established, other personnel expenses are relatively stable in terms of forecasting. A combination of federal and state tax law, along with archdiocesan/diocesan policies and programs, dictate many aspects of these expenses. Below are some common personnel expenses.

FICA: Social Security and Medicare

On payroll stubs, you will often see the acronym *FICA* (Federal Insurance Contributions Act). This charge is the combination of payroll taxes for Social Security and Medicare programs.

Social Security is a national program that provides monthly payments to retired and disabled workers. Medicare is a national health care insurance program that covers all employees under the Social Security system. Hospital insurance (Medicare) is provided to all eligible workers. Both employers and employees contribute to these programs as a percent of gross wages.

St. Michael's contributes 6.2 percent of employee wages for social security and 1.45 percent of employee salary for Medicare.[2]

Workers Compensation/Disability/Unemployment Insurance

Additional payroll expenses that the parish bears include workers compensation, disability, and unemployment insurance. Federal guidelines and in some cases state tax rates form the basis for these expenses. In many dioceses, the cost for these expenses are billed by the diocese.

Medical Insurance

A major benefit provided to employees is access to health insurance or a health maintenance organization. The costs of these plans are usually split between the employer and employee. This has become an increasingly expensive benefit for parishes. Most parishes adopt the medical insurance plan established by the local diocese.

Employee Retirement/Pension

Retirement and pension benefits have evolved significantly over the decades. There are two main types of plans: defined benefits and defined contributions. A **defined benefit plan** is when the employer guarantees the employee a certain benefit under certain conditions. Commonly known as a pension plan, this type of plan has been reduced or eliminated at many organizations because of the risk and long-term costs on employers. The more common and most likely plan that your diocese offers is a

2. Note that contribution rates are subject to federal laws. Refer to the United States Internal Revenue Service for current rates and additional information (www.irs.gov).

defined contribution plan for employees. In this type of plan, the employer contributes a set percent of the employee's salary to an independent investment pool. The employee also has the opportunity to contribute to a plan pretax (up to certain limits).

St. Michael's pays into the Lay Employee Diocesan plan and is
billed at 3 percent of the employee's salary.

Diocesan Assessment

Every parish is assessed a proportion of their annual income for the support of the local diocese. The percentage is established by the local bishop and varies diocese to diocese.

In the diocese where St. Michael's is located, the parish pays
an assessment of 10 percent of total offertory income.

Other Parish Expenses

Given the wide variety of other expenses that a church incurs, we want to highlight five actions you can take to formulate projections for any expense.

1. In a specific expense category, collect financial information for what was budgeted and the actual outlay of resources for the category.

2. Calculate the difference between the two amounts (variance).

3. If there is a variance, what special circumstances or driving factors caused the variance?

4. Do any of these factors impact the upcoming fiscal year? If so, adjust the amount budgeted for the category to account for the change.

5. If no previous budget exists for a specific category, seek information from other parishes, nonprofit organizations, or service providers to understand the costs related to a budget category. For example, if you are initiating the new vacation Bible school, contact another parish that has already conducted this type of program.

Capital Expenses

Expanding upon the discussion in chapter 3, the capital budget is the funding plan for updating, repairing, maintaining, or purchasing assets whose value extends beyond a one-year window. As reflected in the St. Michael's budget, capital funds have been established for renovations to the parish hall, parking lot upgrades, improvements to the church or rectory facilities (e.g., new windows, heating and air conditioning system), money set aside for new equipment purchases (e.g., copier or snow blower), or special funds designated for a specific purpose (e.g., church sound system). When developing the capital budget, consider the variety of assets that will span multiple years and the repairs, maintenance, or replacement they might need.

From a financing perspective, the money used to fund these areas may come from borrowing money from the archdiocese/diocese or bank, capital campaigns, or targeted collections for specific purposes.

Step 4: Present and Finalize

After you collect data, prioritize your time, and develop forecasts, you are ready to compile the master budget. Remember that the master budget includes operating income and expenses, capital expenditures, assumptions, and any additional narrative needed to clarify or explain budget elements.

St. Michael's operating budget has been formatted as a twelve-month income and spending plan for the upcoming fiscal year. Note that income and spending categories that have a consistent cash flow throughout the year are equally divided across the months. For categories that have anticipated fluctuations in cash, the estimates are allocated according to the assumptions that have been developed.

Table 5-11
St. Michael's cash flow budget

To view St. Michael's Cash Flow Budget in its entirety, go to:
www.paulistpress.com, click on Online Resources, and select *Parish Finance*.

Now that the cash flow budget is compiled, let's conclude with some tips for developing an effective forecast.

1. Be careful not to overestimate income or underestimate expenses.

2. Use historical data—information on what *actually* happened is a good foundation for what *might* happen.

3. Forecasts are educated estimates for what we *assume* will happen, not necessarily what will happen.

4. Visualize data and look for patterns or trends to help you understand the present and plan for the future.

5. Perfection and forecasting do not go hand in hand. Go forward one step at a time.

Feedback and Finalization

We began the budget formulation phase with the goal of transparency and collaboration. Now we will conclude the same objective. When communicating the preliminary budget to others, complementing the more detailed cash flow budget, we recommend you create a summarized version for review by the parish community.

Creating this budget summary does not have to be a complex undertaking. We recommend producing a very short, concise document or slide presentation that includes the following:

- Summary of the high-level income and expense categories
- Visualizations (pie charts, bar graphs, etc.) that you believe will help convey information
- Narrative description(s) for additional information and details on new programs, major changes in the budget from previous years, or upcoming financial challenges. Transparency at this stage of budget formulation will pay huge dividends in terms of buy-in and trust by your parishioners of your stewardship capabilities.

Based on feedback received, necessary adjustments can be made and a revised version prepared for the finance council for review and approval. Once approved by the finance council, the budget is ready for submission to the diocese.

Chapter Summary

Building the budget is manageable when you break the process down into component parts. Begin by collecting all pertinent information in terms of policies, procedures, and pastoral documents. Export and review financial data "actuals" from the previous twelve months and familiarize yourself with major income and expense categories. Next, prioritize where you will focus your time on the budget by reviewing the categories that drive the greatest percentage of total income and expenses. After reviewing the data and growing comfortable with your planned income and expense projections, you are ready to consolidate the information. Create a cash flow budget to understand the fluctuations of cash in and out of the budget, and develop a summary document for socialization of the preliminary budget. Once feedback is obtained, you are ready to make any adjustment of, finalize, and submit the budget to your diocese for review.

The good news is that this process truly gets easier over time. As you become more familiar with the elements of the budget (categories, accounts, nuances) you will become even more adept at understanding the financial activities at the parish.

Great job, you did it, the budget has been formulated and you are ready for the fiscal year to begin! In chapter 6, we move to this next phase of the budget process—budget execution.

References

Godevenos, Ken B. *Human Resources for the Church: Applying Corporate Practices in a Spiritual Setting.* Belleville, Ontario: Essence, 2009.

Hanke, John E., Arthur G. Reitsch, and Dean W. Wichern. *Business Forecasting.* 7th ed. Upper Saddle River, NJ: Prentice Hall, 2001.

Laseter, Tim, Casey Lichtendahl, and Yael Grushka-Cockayne. "Cleaning the Crystal Ball: How Intelligent Forecasting Can Lead to Better Decision Making." *Strategy and Business* 59 (Summer 2010): 26–31.

Levine, David M., David Stephan, Timothy C. Krehbiel, and Mark L. Benson, eds. *Statistics for Managers Using Microsoft Excel.* 7th ed. Upper Saddle River, NJ: Prentice Hall, 2014.

United States Conference of Catholic Bishops (USCCB). *Co-workers in the Vineyard of the Lord.* Washington, DC: USCCB, 2005.

Section II

Budget Execution and Control

Chapter 6

Budget Execution

Ready, Set, Go

Chapter 6 Preview

In this chapter, we help Fr. Dave to do the following:

- Understand effective budget execution policies and procedures
- Create payment standards
- Develop and implement a parish expense requisition process
- Learn the variety of types of methods for distributing parish funds
  - Advances, reimbursements, cash disbursement
- Learn key terminology
  - Budget authority
  - Apportionment
  - Purchase orders
  - Invoicing
  - Payment terms

St. Michael's Parish—A New Fiscal Year Begins

Fr. Dave looks down at the calendar and the date is July 1: the new fiscal year has officially begun! The budget has been approved, the team is on board and excited, and Fr. Dave could not be happier. Even though the budget formulation phase this year was "trial by fire," the procedures and processes that were put in place will provide a repeatable, transferable, and refined process in the future.

Fr. Dave decides to take a few days off for the Fourth of July and heads to the beach for a long weekend. Mary is going to wait a few weeks for her vacation because, with the fiscal year ending June 30, she is now in the process of "closing the books" and will start preparing the financial statements for Fr. Dave and the finance council to review in a few weeks.

When Fr. Dave returns to the office on Monday morning, he is faced with a ton of e-mails and a stack of mail. The good news is that the collaborative and comprehensive budget that he and the team put together have set him up for a smooth transition to the next phase of the budget lifecycle—execution.

Budget Execution Policies and Procedures

Execution is the budget phase when the budget plan is put into action. Fr. Dave and the team spent so much time developing the budget; now he wants to make sure that the financial plan put in place is executed well.

Establishing policies and procedures around the collection and disbursement of funds by *all members* of the organization will create a culture of accountability and communication. Accountability is created because all members of the team have clear rules for how money is requested to pay the bills. No one can be exempt from the process or the system will be flawed. As we will discuss further in chapter 8, "Establishing Internal Financial Controls," a minor infraction of the policy can create major financial impacts in the future. If someone or some part of the organization is exempt, this can lead to distrust of the system and at worst, fraud. In terms of communication, the goal is to create a process that has clear roles, responsibilities, and actions.

Following, we outline some suggested strategies that can be used to implement the budget efficiently and effectively. Done well, these techniques will save time, stress, and financial sanity. Budget execution also brings freedom to the leadership team, freedom to focus on the elements of the budget that matter most, as well as provide the most efficient management over the financial plans and goals that the parish has established. Remember, you can always scale these procedures to fit the size of your parish; however, the foundational principles remain the same regardless of size.

Execution Terminology

You may be saying, "More terminology? Will it never end?" Before we jump into this section, let's pause for a moment and recap a key principle in this book—define all terms. We firmly believe that if leaders are clear about terminology, and everyone on the team is speaking the same language, it will help bring clarity to all components of the budget process. Otherwise, when you use a word that others are unfamiliar with, they may *think* or *act* under the assumption that you mean one thing, when in fact you may mean something different. For example, below we describe the terms *budget authority*, *budget apportionment*, *requisition forms*, *purchase orders*, and so on. In many cases, there is not one standard, universal definition for these terms; therefore, providing a simple definition and clear instructions will really help. Remember one of the budget rules of thumb—*be clear about terms and definitions and provide adequate instructions*. This will pay huge dividends in all aspects of managing the parish finances because clarity and understanding equals efficiency!

Budget Authority and Apportionment

In the budget execution phase, you'll hear budgeters refer to the approved amount of funding for a given program or category as "budget authority." Think of **budget authority** as the ceiling above which a program or category of spending cannot pass for a given fiscal year. With a financial goal to ensure that cash is on hand and available for spending throughout a given period, you'll also hear the term **apportionment. Budget apportionment** is a structured process to release funds at specific time periods throughout the fiscal year.

The two concepts of budget authority and apportionment work together for the purposes of budget execution. It provides program managers a total funding *ceiling*, as well as the amount of money *available* for spending for a *given period*. The authority/apportionment tactic helps program managers keep track of how much money is available during a given period of time and answer the question, "How are we doing on our budget?"

St. Michael's Music Program

The music program has an approved annual budget (authority) of twenty thousand dollars. For the first half of the fiscal year, ten thousand has been apportioned.

Establishing an apportionment structure can be very helpful, especially for parishes that deal with uneven cash flow. Apportionment provides clear guidelines on how much money is available for a specific program or spending line item for a given period. Some may argue that apportionment is "management controlling staff." However, a better way to describe this process is to say, "Apportionment is not intended to control staff but to *control spending*." Key benefits of this structure include the following:

- Helping members of the team who may not be as familiar with managing budgets to easily understand how much money is available for spending on a program area
- Limiting the amount of money available so all is not spent at the beginning of a new fiscal year before assumptions have been validated
- Ensuring that cash is available for spending during given periods, given actual income and spending targets
- Understanding the specific, predetermined dates that have been established for availability of funds

Apportionment Guidelines

Apportionment can be implemented using the cash flow budget as the blueprint for when money is distributed. The process can be made simple:

- As part of the budget process, program staff developed estimates for spending categories by month. (Note: see the benefits of staff involvement! If staff has put the budget together, they already know how much money they have budgeted and can manage to that budget.)
- Break the fiscal year into quarters or biannual periods.
    - Q1 (July–September), Q2 (October–December), Q3 (January–March), Q4 (April–June)

    or

    - Period 1 (July–December), Period 2 (January–June)
- Review the approved cash flow budget and divide the budget for each program into their respective estimates for the established period (quarterly or biannually)
    - At St. Michael's, the CCD program may need to buy books in August, so more money may be available in the first quarter than in the fourth quarter of the fiscal year. Alternately, the music ministry budget is broken out evenly for the four quarters.
- Use an apportionment memo or other means to inform all members of the staff how much money is available for the given quarter for their program area.
    - CCD Program—Q1 available budget is $2,574
    - Music Program—Q1 available budget is $5,000
- As each quarter approaches, validate that the budget assumptions created during the budget process have been met and release or reduce funds for the next

---

apportionment period depending on the circumstances. Unsure how to make this determination? We will discuss the use of variance analysis in chapter 7 to analyze income and spending to help you get the answer.

- Collections are down by 3 percent in the first quarter and Mary (business manager) wants to ensure that enough resources are available for Q2 as the parish prepares for Advent and Christmas. Because the Christmas collection will not be known until the end of the quarter, Mary has asked each program to be more conservative with expenses in the second quarter until there is more information on whether the pattern of decreasing collections will continue.

In summary, each program area can have budget authority (ceiling) for the given fiscal year, but money flows through an apportionment process.

If the apportionment process seems burdensome for a smaller parish, you can scale the process down to meet your needs. The key criteria to determine whether you implement an apportionment process at your parish is whether your cash flow is "bumpy," resulting in "cash flow issues" throughout the year, or if you are seeking more control over spending. If your parish finds itself in a position where funding is more limited at certain times of the year and the income and spending at the parish is highly dependent on sensitive factors, an apportionment process can help create additional stability.

The Parish Expense Requisition Form

Creating a standard template for the disbursement of funds can be extremely helpful for budget execution. The benefits of having staff complete a standard form are numerous, including the following:

- Establishing controls to the allocation for how money is distributed, for what purpose, and to whom. *Chapter 8 provides more information on internal controls.*
- Opening communication on the management team as to what is being purchased
- Providing a standard operating procedure so that all members of the team know what is expected in terms of money outflows

A **parish requisition form** can be used to disburse funds. All members of the staff, and parishioners involved in receiving parish funds, must complete a standard form to spend or commit parish funds. You can adapt this form to meet any specific needs at your parish. Although the key elements of a requisition form may seem intuitive, the items below are essential, regardless of the complexity of the form you create. Your parish financial management software may include templates for this type of information, or you can create a simple template as demonstrated in figure 6-1.

Figure 6-1
Template: Parish expense requisition form

Requested By: _____ Date: _____

Request Type: □ Expense Authorization *(Complete Part A)*

□ Check Request *(Complete Parts A and B)*
    □ Advance   □ Reimbursement
□ Cash *(Complete Parts A and B)*
Budget Line Item/Category *(If applicable)*:

Part A - Expense Authorization:
Details: **Amount**

_____   _____
_____   _____

_____   _____

Justification:
Please provide any justification in the space provided
Additional comments can be made on the back of this form
Part B - Payment Details *(If applicable)*:
Payee Name: _____
Payee Address: _____

_____

Please let us know how payment is to be received:
    □ Office Pick Up   □ Mailed to Payee
Special Instructions:

_____   _____
Submitter Signature   *Date*

Additional Comments

For Office Use Only

Authorization

_____   _____
Authorization Signature   *Date*

_____   _____
Authorization Signature   *Date*
For all expenses over $250, two signatures are required

Please allow 3 to 5 business days for approvals
Thank you! For any questions, please contact the Parish Office.

Elements of the Requisition Form

Even if templates exist, we can help you become familiar with the essential elements so that you can explain to others not only the "how to" of requesting funds but also the "why" that makes these elements important.

1. **Name/Date**—Include the name of the person making the submission and the date submitted to create a tracking date.

2. **Type of Request**—Include the type of request approval/disapproval. Options may include a request to commit money for a specific purpose, seek an advance check, a reimbursement check, or cash.

3. **Budget Category/Line Item**—Following the guidance in earlier chapters, staff should be aware of the budget that has been approved. Therefore, when applicable, have the submitter include the budget program area or line item where they believe the funds should be distributed. If they are unsure of the budget category, have them note this on the form. Remember, a main purpose of managing all elements of the budget is to bring awareness of the funds available from the approved budget.

4. **Justification**—Include why the request is being made and for what purpose. Submitters should include only relevant information. Guide them on the type of information you are seeking. If this is a new process to the parish, provide sample templates for common requests.

5. **Amount Requested**—What is the exact amount, in dollars and cents, being requested?

6. **Payment Details**—Who should receive payment? Is this a person (staff member), organization (local charity), store?

7. **Submitter's Signature**—Ensure that the submitter signs the form to validate the information in the form.

8. **Approver's Signatures**—Include who will be able to authorize the payment.

The first part of the form should outline the request that is being made. This part of the form answers the questions, "Who is requesting funds?" "For what purpose(s) are the funds to be spent?" The second part of the form will answer, "How will the funds be disbursed?" As stated previously, if your staff is new to this form, put some easy-to-follow instructions at the top of the form to help guide them. Following are the varieties of types of requests that can be made on the parish requisition form.

Expense Authorization

Authorization for spending parish funds should always be submitted for approval to the parish business office. What process will you establish for approving funding requests? As we stated above, include the authorized approver on the requisition form. This ensures that clear roles and responsibilities are established for the approval of each type of request. As we discuss further in chapter 8 on internal controls, you will want to establish multiple accountability layers.

Criteria

Establish criteria for the approval process. For example, a reimbursement for pizza may only require review of the attached receipt. However, an advance check request for a major purchase may require additional justification.

Check Requests

Check requests are standard procedures at most parishes for the purposes of issuing checks for advances, commitments (obligations), or reimbursements. Let's review each type.

Advances

Once an expense has been approved, an advance check can be issued for an exact amount of money that will be used for a specific purpose. An advance check can also be used to fulfill a commitment or obligation that has been made for a specific purpose. An *obligation* is any amount of funding that may require payment at a future time by the parish.

St. Michael's

- Michele (faith formation) is hosting a speaker and would like to give her the stipend check on the day she arrives for the presentation.
- Ron has gone online and ordered sheet music to be picked up at the store. The music store does not require payment until pick-up, so St. Michael's has made an obligation to pay for the sheet music at that time. Once the check is issued by the parish business office, Ron can use it when he goes to the store to pick up the music.

Reimbursements

Reimbursements are common in parishes. The key to any type of reimbursement request is to ensure that the paperwork is complete, all receipts are attached, and there are controls established to ensure the legitimacy of any reimbursements distributed.

Cash

Cash in the form of *advances* or *reimbursements* should be used on a limited basis. Establishing clear ground rules around cash is critical to the budget execution process. Cash as a form of payment or receipt must be clearly tracked and accounted for at all times because it has a high risk of fraudulent activity.

As a form of *advance payment*, cash should only be considered when all other forms of payment, such as check or credit card, cannot be accepted. Examples may include a parishioner taking a group on a service trip who would like to use cash for tolls, or the parish youth director bringing students to a theme park who would like to give each child fifteen dollars to buy snacks.

Provided the management team approves the expense, the cash advance may also be used when the parish credit card is unavailable. For example, a non–staff member, who will not have access to a parish credit card, needs money for a specific purpose. This can also help control the amount of money that is spent for a specific purpose. An example is a parishioner who is leading a trip and will need cash to tip the bus driver.

Another option to limit the use of petty cash is allowing individuals to use personal funds and seek reimbursement from the parish by submitting a check request. All of these options assume that the management team has approved the expenses. You would not want a parishioner to go out and buy one hundred dollars' worth of flowers for Easter and expect a cash reimbursement when the expense was not approved.

If petty cash is used, clear and accurate records must be kept to ensure that all transactions are legitimate. Advance cash payments are very difficult to track without receipts. Whether cash is used for advances or reimbursements, receipts must be submitted for all transactions. Table 6-1 displays a sample petty cash disbursement log where the information can be recorded and tracked.

Table 6-1
Template: Petty cash disbursement log

St. Michael's Petty Cash Distribution					
Balance	Date	Purpose	Approved Signature	Debit (Subtract)	Credit (Add)

Receipts and Supporting Documentation

An established policy must be set regarding the necessity of receipts and supporting documentation for all payments. Without a receipt, or supporting document (in the case of an advance) or proof of purchase, a check reimbursement will not be approved.

St. Michael's—A Snowblower in August?

Joe (maintenance manager) has always been considered a rock star at the parish for his work ethic and skills. Joe is responsible for the maintenance of all parish buildings and grounds. From plumbing, electrical work, painting, equipment repair, event setup, and keeping the parish clean and orderly, he does it all. Another major role that Joe plays at the parish is managing the contracted services for lawn care and ice and snow removal.

Joe had put the acquisition of a snowblower as a possible purchase in the capital equipment budget for the upcoming year. Even though the overall budget was approved, there were no guidelines in the budget for *when* the purchase was to be made. So, when Joe saw some great deals on snowblowers he decided, "What better time than now to start looking?" He runs through his list of requirements and then shops around. After reading the online reviews and going to a few stores to look at them, he decides on a gas-powered snowblower for $799. Prior to making the purchase, Joe pulls up the parish requisition form and fills it out. He writes a brief justification on why this particular snowblower will work well and includes some comparative pricing. He also addresses why he wants to buy the snowblower in August: "Even though it's only August, we'll get a better deal now. Let's not wait until the first winter storm; then it will cost more."

Joe submits the requisition form to the office to be reviewed by Mary. Mary reviews the forms, checks that the money is available for use, and signs the requisition form. Because the amount is over $250, she also gives the form to Fr. Dave, who reviews and approves it. To simplify this process, Mary approves Joe to use the parish credit card to make the purchase. Now that both have signed off, Joe goes to the store and purchases the snowblower. When he comes back to the office, he submits the receipt and warranty information for the parish files.

Reflection Question:
Can you brainstorm some of the benefits that this process brings to the staff at St. Michael's?

Possible responses include the following:

1. *Communication*—How often have you either heard or asked the question, "I didn't know we bought a new _____ for the parish?" The team is now aware that the parish has a snowblower. This process can help open communication.

2. *Financial management*—Mary can make the accounting entries and reduce the available funds for this line item in the budget.

3. *Staff empowerment*—Joe feels empowered. Not only is he prepared for the winter, but he is looking forward to using the new equipment.

4. *Succession planning*—In three years, if Joe, Mary, and Fr. Dave have moved on, the paperwork detailing the rationale and specifics of the purchase will remain. This provides future parish staff the ability to understand the purchase.

Other Execution Formats
Purchase Orders

Purchase Orders are typically required when a contract exists with a vendor to buy supplies, materials, or other items that require large expenditures. This type of form is generated by the parish financial manager or bookkeeper and approved through the same format above. You can usually generate this form directly from your accounting software.

Invoicing

Invoices are the format in which payment is requested by vendors or contractors. A standard invoice includes the details necessary for payment to be made by the parish. Elements of a standard invoice include date, price of goods or services, and quantity or amount.

Payment Terms

Following is a quick orientation to common payment terms that are used by vendors or service providers, and can be used by the parish when seeking payment.

Due Upon Receipt

The meaning of *due upon receipt* is intuitive, but to clarify, it is a standard term used by a service provider to make clear when payment is expected. Unless another payment term has been worked out, the parish will likely want to use *due upon receipt* for all standard invoices. This means that vendors should issue an invoice on the date the service or item is received. This helps with cash flow because the parish is not providing flexibility to vendors and service providers on when payment should be expected.

Net # Days

You will also see in payment details **Net # days**. This is a standard payment term that means that the purchaser of goods must pay the seller on or before the # (number) of calendar days from which the goods or services were obtained. Terms can also include *Net 10* or *Net 15* and in rare cases *Net 60*. You will often see this term used when a contractor or service provider allows a discount to be applied to the total cost of payment under certain terms. For example, a service provider might say that payment is due in full in *Net 30* but if payment is made within ten days, a 3 percent discount will be applied. This means that if the parish pays the invoice within ten calendar days, the parish will pay 3 percent less and the service provider receives payment sooner than thirty days. Both benefit from this transaction. The service provider receives money quicker (helping with cash flow) and the parish benefits from receiving a discount by paying for the services in a timely fashion.

Chapter Summary

Budget execution is the phase when the plan becomes a reality. As collections are received and expenses paid, the execution policies and procedures put into place will ensure smooth parish operations. Budget execution strategies include apportioning money to help manage cash flow, creating a clear and understandable parish expense requisition process, and developing efficient payment and processing procedures. Combined, these tactics offer the parish a structured and effective approach to resource management.

Now that we have discussed an overview of budget execution policies and procedures, in chapter 7, we will turn to the subject of budget controls and how they can help you stay on track and, if necessary, get you back on track, with parish finances.

Chapter 7

Budget Controls

Staying on Track

Chapter 7 Preview

In this chapter, we help Fr. Dave to do the following:

- Establish a budget control checkpoint process to focus on the overall health of the parish finances
- Learn how to use variance reports to analyze differences between the budgeted and actual amounts of money received or spent
- Conduct a comprehensive budget analysis by using a QUEST (Question, Understand, Estimate, Solve, Track) strategy
- Address financial challenges and make any necessary adjustments

St. Michael's Parish—Budget versus Actuals

It is October 1 and three months have passed since the start of the fiscal year. Fr. Dave can't believe how quickly time has gone and his attention turns again to finances. He wants to understand how the parish is doing financially and is not sure how to go about it.

Fr. Dave asks Mary to pull together some information for him. She sends him the following e-mail:

> **To: Fr. Dave**
> **From: Mary**
> **Date: October 1**
> **Re: Budget Actuals**
>
> Hi Fr. Dave,
>
> I reviewed the budget information. We seem to be doing OK, except that collections are down about 3 percent from last summer. I think this is largely due to the beautiful summer! It was so nice; I think more people went away on vacation than last summer, causing the collections to go down. We also seem to have some money left in categories like programs and plant/facilities, but have underbudgeted administrative/office and liturgical/sacramental expenses. Let's meet and review the numbers.
>
> Thanks,
> Mary
> St. Michael's Business Manager

Fr. Dave's fears of managing parish finances return. He understands that the budget is off, but he doesn't know how this impacts the overall budget. He wonders, "We have so much going on at the parish right now, how do I focus on what to do next? What actions do we need to take to correct the budget? How do I make sure this doesn't happen again?"

Budget Controls to Manage and Safeguard Parish Resources

St. Michael's is not unique in that budgets are not written in stone and forecasts are predictions and sometimes not perfectly accurate. However, there are tools available to assist Fr. Dave in keeping the budget on track.

For the next two chapters, we will focus on two aspects of budget controls—managing ongoing financial operations and safeguarding parish assets. In this chapter, we assist Fr. Dave to ensure that the parish "stays on track" between budgeted and actual results. In chapter 8, we discuss how effective financial controls also safeguard parish assets.

Budget controls work together to manage the inflows and outflows of parish resources. To establish the budget control process, there are two main steps. First, Fr. Dave will mark specific dates during the fiscal year as *budget control checkpoints*. Second, using a tool known as a **variance analysis**, he'll review the difference between budgeted amounts and actual amounts and analyze the results.

By creating a dashboard, the variance between budgeted and actual amounts per category of income and expenses is easily calculated and displayed for a given period. This could be a year, a quarter, or six months, but the key is that you have data available.

Step 1: Determine Checkpoint Dates

Fr. Dave will begin by establishing checkpoint dates for when the variance analysis will be conducted and the period being reviewed. Whether you are reviewing budgeted and actual results for a week, month, quarter, or year, it helps to have a specific date on which the results will be reported, reviewed, and analyzed. If you are new to budgeting, you may want to start by reviewing data monthly to become comfortable with the categories of income and expenses and the financial inflows and outflows of resources. As time goes on, you can move to a quarterly process. Like many topics in this book, begin by understanding the overall method and then you can rightsize the process to fit your organization's needs.

Figure 7-1 below displays a sample quarterly budget control checkpoint process.

Figure 7-1
Sample budget control checkpoints

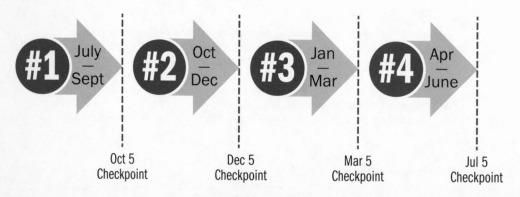

#1 July – Sept	#2 Oct – Dec	#3 Jan – Mar	#4 Apr – June
Oct 5 Checkpoint	Dec 5 Checkpoint	Mar 5 Checkpoint	Jul 5 Checkpoint

Step 2: Create a Variance Report

Once the quarterly review checkpoint has arrived, all income and expense data can be exported from your financial management software and reviewed in a variance report. This report is the tool you'll use to review, analyze, and take action based on the difference between the budget and actual income and expenditures.

Creating a variance analysis report is an intuitive process. Parish management software can prepopulate templates to generate and view this information. However, to help you understand this report, we detail below the specific elements to generate it on your own.

Variance Report Elements

As shown in table 7-1 below, variance report elements are displayed and include the required data, the sources of the information, and the applicable calculations.

Table 7-1
Variance report template

	A	B	C	D	E
	Budget Category	**Budgeted Amount ($)**	**Actual Amount ($)**	**Variance Amount ($)**	**Variance Percentage (%)**
		From DATE to DATE	From DATE to DATE	From DATE to DATE	From DATE to DATE
Income					
Information Source / Calculation	Budget Line Items	Cash Flow Budget	Export Income Financial Data	Actual (C) - Budget (B)	Variance (D) ÷ Budgeted (B)
Expenses					
Information Source / Calculation	Budget Line Items	Cash Flow Budget	Export Expense Financial Data	Budget (B) - Actual (C)	Variance (D) ÷ Budgeted (B)

Let's review the variance report elements.

> **A. Budget Category** is the income or spending category you are analyzing.
>
> *Action*: Using the budget you have formulated, enter the categories you are reviewing. We suggest you begin by creating the variance analysis with the higher-level categories (1000 Collections, 2300 Administrative/Office). After reviewing the results, you can be more specific with those items you would like to investigate in more detail (1001 Sunday Collections, 1002 Holy Day Collections, 2301 Supplies and Equipment).
>
> **B. Budgeted Amount ($)** is the total amount of money you have budgeted for the category for the given time period you are reviewing.
>
> *Action*: Using the cash flow budget, total the sum per category for the period you are analyzing. For example, if you are conducting a variance analysis from July 1 through October 1, use the cash flow budget to add the amounts per category for July, August, and September.
>
> **C. Actual Amount ($)** is the amount of money that was actually received or spent for the analysis period.

Action: Export the data from your financial management software for the analysis period.

D. Variance Amount ($) is the amount difference between the budgeted amount and actual amount.

Action: For *income* categories, subtract the budgeted amount (B) from actual amount (C) that has been received as income. A positive number indicates that more income was received than budgeted, whereas a negative number indicates that less money was received than budgeted. For *expense categories*, subtract the actual amount (C) from the budgeted amount (B). For expenses, a negative result indicates that expenses have exceeded the budgeted amount (overspent), whereas a positive number indicates that less money has been spent than budgeted.

E. Variance Percentage (%) is the percent difference between the budget and actual income and expenses per category.

Action: Calculate the variance percentage for both income and expense categories by dividing the variance amount (D) by the budgeted amount (B).

Now that the template is created, you can quickly calculate the variances, analyze the information, and discuss needed actions. Table 7-2 is the quarterly report generated for St. Michael's. Note that the report indicates the analysis period is for July 1 through September 30, the first three months of the fiscal year.

Table 7-2
St. Michael's variance analysis
July 1–September 30

A	B	C	D	E
Budget Category	**Budget Amount ($)**	**Actual Amount ($)**	**Variance Amount ($)**	**Variance Percentage (%)**
	From July 1 to Sept. 30	**From July 1 to Sept. 30**	**From July 1 to Sept. 30**	**From July 1 to Sept. 30**
Income				
1000 Collections	$160,456	$155,642	**-$4,814**	-3%
1100 Donations	$3,500	$3,650	$150	4%
1200 Programs	$4,250	$4,300	$50	1%
1300 Other Income	$3,500	$3,600	$100	3%
Total Income	$171,706	$167,192	**-$4,514**	-3%
Expenses				
2000 Personnel/Salary	$45,500	$45,500	$0	0%
2100 Personnel/Other	$20,072	$19,250	$822	4%
2200 Diocesan Assess.	$0	$0	$0	0%
2300 Admin./Office	$18,745	$20,150	**-$1,405**	-7%
2400 Lit./Sacramental	$10,245	$11,250	**-$1,005**	-10%
2500 Programs	$15,755	$15,000	$755	5%
2600 Plant/Facilities	$28,925	$27,000	$1,925	7%
Total Expenses	$139,242	$138,150	$1,092	1%

Determine Thresholds

Now that the variance amount and percentage have been calculated, you can focus the analysis on those variances that are having the biggest impact on your budget.

Your goal is to understand serious deviations versus minor short-term problems. One method that you can use to visualize thresholds and quickly interpret data is to evaluate each category using a rating scale and assign an icon or color to display the status of the budget category. Threshold amounts will depend on your budget. For example, an 8 percent difference on a $2 million budget may not be as problematic as the impact it could have on a $400,000 budget. When determining the thresholds, ask yourself the question, "Given the size of our parish budget, what negative (or positive) amount and percentage will indicate whether the budgeted amount versus actual amount will have a significant, possible, or limited impact?" Figure 7-2 displays a sample rating scale with some common budget thresholds.

Figure 7-2

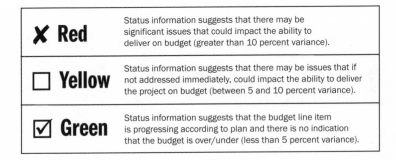

✘ Red	Status information suggests that there may be significant issues that could impact the ability to deliver on budget (greater than 10 percent variance).
☐ Yellow	Status information suggests that there may be issues that if not addressed immediately, could impact the ability to deliver the project on budget (between 5 and 10 percent variance).
☑ Green	Status information suggests that the budget line item is progressing according to plan and there is no indication that the budget is over/under (less than 5 percent variance).

Sample variance analysis thresholds and status icons

In table 7-3, we have added a status column (F) in the St. Michael's variance report and scored each category against the thresholds we established above.[1]

Table 7-3
St. Michael's variance analysis with status icons
July 1–September 30

A	B	C	D	E	F
Budget Category	**Budget Amount ($)**	**Actual Amount ($)**	**Variance Amount ($)**	**Variance Percentage (%)**	**Status**
	From July 1 to Sept. 30	From July 1 to Sept. 30	From July 1 to Sept. 30	From July 1 to Sept. 30	From July 1 to Sept. 30
Income					
1000 Collections	$160,456	$155,642	**-$4,814**	**-3%**	☑ Green
1100 Donations	$3,500	$3,650	$150	4%	☑ Green
1200 Programs	$4,250	$4,300	$50	1%	☑ Green
1300 Other Income	$3,500	$3,600	$100	3%	☑ Green

Table 7-3 continued on next page

Table 7-3 continued on next page

---

1. To add status icons in the variance analysis template, you can use your spreadsheet software's conditional formatting option to create this display.

Table 7-3 continued

Total Income	$171,706	$167,192	-$4,514	-3%	☑ Green
A	**B**	**C**	**D**	**E**	**F**
Budget Category	Budget Amount ($)	Actual Amount ($)	Variance Amount ($)	Variance Percentage (%)	Status
From July 1 to September 30					
2000 Personnel/ Salary	$45,500	$45,500	$0	0%	☑ Green
2100 Personnel/ Other	$20,072	$19,250	$822	4%	☑ Green
2200 Diocesan Assess.	$0	$0	$0	0%	☑ Green
2300 Admin./Office	$18,745	$20,150	**-$1,405**	**-7%**	☐ Yellow
2400 Lit./ Sacramental	$10,245	$11,250	**-$1,005**	**-10%**	✘ Red
2500 Programs	$15,755	$15,000	$755	5%	☑ Green
2600 Plant/Facilities	$28,925	$27,000	$1,925	7%	☑ Green
Total Expenses	$139,242	$138,150	$1,092	1%	☑ Green
Income/Expense Variance Gap			**-$3,422**		

St. Michael's

Fr. Dave quickly reviews the variance report. By viewing the status column (F), he can focus his attention on those categories that are the most variant. As he already heard from Mary, collections are in fact down 3 percent. Expenses are also more than anticipated for administrative/office and liturgical/sacramental estimates. These categories are showing variances of 7 percent and 10 percent, respectively. When the total variances are summarized for both income and expenses, we see that St. Michael's is showing a gap between income and expenses of negative $3,422. Fr. Dave ponders a number of concerning questions: "What will the impact of the variances have short and long term?" "Did we miscalculate a category of spending?" "Are the assumptions we created inaccurate?"

The short answer to these questions is—we need more information!

Analyze Results

When confronted with the challenge of what to do when income or expenses are higher or lower than planned, often we do not take the adequate time to probe further to uncover underlying factors that are driving results. The answer may not be black or white. Budget analysis is like peeling an onion. Peel the onion one layer at a time and begin by asking questions and gathering information.

We like to use the acronym **QUEST** to help you to uncover, focus, and respond to changing circumstances surrounding your budget plan. We will use the example at St. Michael's to illustrate the concepts.

> **Q = Question**
> **U = Understand**
> **E = Evaluate**
> **S = Solve**
> **T = Track**

Q = Question

Gather data and information, and discuss the situation with the team to arrive at the next level of understanding. This is not an attempt to put blame on people or circumstances for variances but to open communication and share accountability.

Begin by focusing on the categories that are having the most impact on the overall budget. In the example for St. Michael's, we'll dive further into the variances in administrative and sacramental.

As a first step, Fr. Dave can ask Mary, who is intimately familiar with parish income and expenses due to her role as business manager, if she has any information why collections income is down and costs are higher than planned for specific categories. Through this discussion, Fr. Dave discovers that although liturgical/sacramental expenses are 10 percent higher than planned, Mary was able to secure a 10 percent discount on supplies if she purchased a six-month supply in advance, instead of quarterly purchases. Therefore, the category appears higher than anticipated during this quarter, but in six months, this expense will actually generate savings.

This example highlights the importance of asking questions before concluding what needs to happen next. Of course, this may also allow Fr. Dave to adjust the budget execution policies for staff to communicate more proactively on these types of items.

However, Fr. Dave was still having difficulty trying to figure out why 2300-Administrative/Office expenses were 7 percent over budget. Sometimes questioning is not enough. The next step in the analysis is to understand and evaluate the data.

UE = Understand and Evaluate

If the question phase of variance analysis gets you through one layer of peeling the onion, understanding helps you to get to the core. After you have compiled information and data, you can now dig deeper into the driving factors or assumptions that underlie your results. Be careful not to skip over this phase without adequately addressing all of the factors that may be moving behind the scenes.

Returning to the higher than expected administrative and office expenses at St. Michael's, Fr. Dave determines that it would be helpful to see some additional details of the 2300-Administrative/Office expenses. As displayed in table 7-4, a variance report is created for this specific category of expenses.

Table 7-4
St. Michaels administrative/office expenses variance analysis

A		B	C	D	E	F
		Budget Amount ($)	Actual Amount ($)	Variance Amount ($)	Variance Percent (%)	Status
Line Item	Budget Category	From July 1 to September 30				
2300 Administrative/Office						
2301	Supplies and Equipment	$1,125	$1,200	-$75	-7%	☐ Yellow
2302	Postage	$750	$800	-$50	-7%	☐ Yellow
2303	Printing and Copying	$2,500	$2,550	-$50	-2%	☑ Green
2304	Offertory Envelopes	$0	$0	$0	0%	☑ Green
2305	Advertising	$400	$400	$0	0%	☑ Green

Table 7-4 continued on next page

Table 7-4 continued

	A	B	C	D	E	F
Line Item	**Budget Category**	**Budget Amount ($)**	**Actual Amount ($)**	**Variance Amount ($)**	**Variance Percent (%)**	**Status**
		From July 1 to September 30				
2300 Administrative/Office						
2307	Security System	$325	$325	$0	0%	☑ Green
2308	Internet	$600	$600	$0	0%	☑ Green
2309	Office Phones	$1,375	$1,375	$0	0%	☑ Green
2310	Cell Phones	$750	$750	$0	0%	☑ Green
2311	Website Support and Development	$0	$0	$0	0%	☑ Green
2312	Automobile and Travel	$2,500	$3,000	-$500	-20%	✗ Red
2313	Priest Reimbursement	$1,125	$1,150	-$25	-2%	☑ Green
2314	Parish Meals and Hosting	$875	$100	$775	89%	☑ Green
2315	Interest and Bank Charges	$250	$150	$100	40%	☑ Green
2316	Criminal Background Checks	$500	$1,600	-$1,100	-220%	✗ Red
2317	Contracted Services	$2,500	$2,500	$0	0%	☑ Green
2318	Extra Clergy Assistance	$1,250	$1,650	-$400	-32%	✗ Red
2319	Fundraising	$545	$0	$545	100%	☑ Green
2320	Parish Hall Supplies	$1,000	$2,000	-$1,000	-100%	✗ Red
	Total Administrative/ Office	**$18,745**	**$20,150**	**-$1,405**	**-7%**	☐ Yellow

Fr. Dave will again use the status column to focus his efforts. He then has additional discussions with staff and finds out more information on the red categories:

2316 Criminal Background Checks (-220 percent, -$1,100)

This line item causes concern because of the impact it is having on the overall variance for the administrative and office category. However, after doing some digging, Fr. Dave recalled that in July, the diocese mandated that criminal background checks be performed on any personnel that associate with children. St. Michael's had paid for the background checks for all staff as well as any volunteers that work with children in any capacity.

2320 Parish Hall Supplies (-100 percent, -$1,000)

Michele (faith formation) wanted to make sure that she had enough supplies for hosting the variety of upcoming fall programs and decided to go to a food and supply discount store and stock up on a six-month supply of items.

2318 Extra Clergy Assistance (-32 percent, -$400)

Although this line item is showing a 32 percent variance, Fr. Dave notes that the cash flow budget is not reflective of the actual expenses related to this category. In fact, summer expenses for extra clergy assistance are usually higher than the rest of the year due to priest vacations.

2312 Automobile and Travel (-20 percent, -$500)

Fr. Dave asks Mary to review the financial records associated with this line item. After examining the credit card statements, Mary discovers that fuel expenses are higher than projected. Fr. Dave also notes that a number of line items have either no expenses (i.e., 2306-Audit and Legal Services) or less money has been spent than budgeted (i.e., 2314-Parish Meals and Hosting).

To further evaluate the categories, Fr. Dave also reviews the Budgeted Category Impact Percentage used in the budget formulation phase to determine the overall impact these categories have on the annual budget. After reviewing the information, talking with staff, and examining budget assumptions, Fr. Dave has additional clarity and is ready to develop some solutions.

S = Solve

Developing a solution to many financial challenges can seem daunting. However, through the question, understand, and evaluate phases, your analysis will likely lead you to translate budget problems into more manageable chunks. Although there are no one-size-fits-all solutions, key questions can be asked to determine the right course of action.

1. What impact does this challenge have on the overall budget?

2. Which stakeholders need to be involved in the solution?

3. How quickly do we need to implement a solution (immediately, zero to three months, six months to one year, long term)?

4. What are the alternative options available to implement?

5. What are the risks to the success of the solution? How can we mitigate these risks?

Addressing Variances

The most immediate, proactive, and likely approach to addressing variances involves making immediate changes to operations to reduce spending in specific areas or increase the amount of income to meet gaps. Determine the extent to which the impact affects the overall budget and then take necessary actions based on this impact.

A second approach to addressing variances involves reallocating (also referred to as reprogramming) funds. You will want to limit the times you undertake a reallocation process so that the budget does not become invalid every time circumstances change. If necessary, we recommend only completing a reallocation process one time throughout the entire fiscal year. **Reallocation** involves adjustments of the budget through the movement of money from one category to another.

When undertaking a reallocation, the best practice is to only make budget adjustments *within* a high-level category, for example, line items contained within administrative/office instead of *between* first-level categories (for example, moving money between administrative/office and personnel). The reason we caution against the reallocation of funds between the higher-level categories is that you will want to ensure the integrity of the budget and not constantly be making adjustments just because circumstances have changed. There are also rules and regulations about the movement of capital funds into operational funds. Review diocesan policies for these matters.

Third, for smaller variances, you can use a "wait and see" approach. This does not mean being passive or unresponsive to variances, but allows time to pass so that you can determine whether variances are general trends or one-off occurrences. With this solution, you'll want to create a specific time period in the future to return to the data. For example, a specific category of income or expenses is reviewed on a monthly basis before the next budget control checkpoint.

St. Michael's

Through his analysis, Fr. Dave is now comfortable with the reasoning behind the increase in expenses for criminal background checks because the majority of checks on staff and volunteers for this year have been completed. However, he does want to address parish hall supplies. Fr. Dave asks Mary to review budget execution policies and determine if any policy changes are needed before staff makes decisions like the one to purchase six month of supplies.

As you can see, during this budget control checkpoint process, Fr. Dave decides to use the "wait and see" approach. At the next budget control checkpoint (October through December), Fr. Dave sees a pattern emerge. An expense related to automobile/travel continues to rise through the first six months. Alternatively, spending related to audit/legal services and parish meals/hosting have been much less than projected. Fr. Dave decides to move funds from audit/legal services and parish meals/hosting into automobile/travel.

After the reallocation process, the budget now more accurately reflects the actual expenses related to these categories. To close out the process, Fr. Dave records the changes that were made so that these factors can be considered in next year's budget formulation phase.

T = Track

The final step is to track actions and results. This phase helps two ways in budget analysis. First, it directs you during periodic checkpoints to ensure that you are meeting your expected results and goals. Second, it provides you with the opportunity to know what success looks like when you have arrived. Tracking can help you stay accountable to your anticipated goals. For example, if you were trying to manage supply costs, you may determine that instead of only reviewing supply costs monthly, for the next quarter, you may consider reviewing these expenses every two weeks. By implementing a tracking process, you answer the question, "Where are we with this item and has anything changed?" This also reduces stress in your organization because you and the team know when you will return to review this item.

Tracking also forces you to answer the question, "What does success look like for our proposed solution?" Organizations often fail to define what success looks like because it can seem overwhelming. To overcome this hurdle, stop trying so hard to make your goals perfect. Draw a line in the sand and see how close you come to meeting your target in an established time. Defining what success looks like for your organization is good practice. Keep goals simple and remember that tracking requires two elements, a goal and a period during which you will measure this goal.

For reducing fuel costs, the goal may be as simple as lowering costs in three months by 3 percent with monthly check-ins to determine progress. Without a clear understanding of what you hope to achieve, it is very difficult to know when you have arrived. Think of measuring success as planning a road trip. If you are trying to get from point A to point B, you may need to see a few road signs along the way to determine how much longer it will take to get to your destination, or if you are heading down the wrong road. Tracking is your GPS for the trip.

The 3-R Response to Errors

Let's face it, sometimes forecasts are incorrect and errors occur. Whether it is a miscalculation or a careless error, mistakes are a reality in every organization. The key is the response. A method you can use to respond to errors or miscalculations is to use what we call the *3-R Approach*. The first step is to *reflect* on what has occurred. What is the actual data telling you about what happened? The second step is to *review* reasons or circumstances that affected the forecast and to consider any changes that may be needed in how you project or estimate amounts in the future. The third step is to *refine* any policies and procedures to mitigate the likelihood that the error will occur again.

Chapter Summary

By setting up a simple budget control checkpoint process, with specific dates to review actual performance against budget plans, you've taken action to keep plans on track. Variance reporting and analysis provide you a quick and easy tool to gain insight on the inflows and outflows of resources. Deploying a program like QUEST can bring you clarity around what may be needed to adjust or recalibrate plans and actions. As you implement the concepts of this chapter, remember that establishing a simple process is better than having no process at all.

In chapter 8, we will discuss how to establish policies and procedures to safeguard assets.

Chapter 8

Establishing Internal Financial Controls

Chapter 8 Preview

In this chapter, we help Fr. Dave to do the following:

- Understand the importance of internal financial controls
- Learn about internal and external audits
- Learn best practices in implementing internal controls
  - The importance of a procedures manual
  - Limiting the number of parish bank accounts
  - Requiring multiple signers of large checks
  - Requiring documentation for all reimbursements
  - Safely handling the weekend collection money
  - Segmentation of duties
- Utilize electronic giving

St. Michael's Parish—The Internal Audit and Actions

The letter from the chancery caught Fr. Dave by surprise. It informed him that, since there had been a change in pastors, diocesan guidelines called for an internal financial audit of St. Michael's. The diocesan auditor would be arriving next month. He was to ensure that the books were in order.

After inquiring, Fr. Dave learned that an **internal audit**, performed by a diocesan staff member, was slightly different from an **external audit**, performed by an outside accounting firm. While both examine and analyze many individual transactions, the external auditor provides an opinion on whether the financial accounts show a true and fair view of the parish's finances. Internal auditors form an opinion on the adequacy and effectiveness of risk management and internal control systems, many of which fall outside the main accounting systems. The primary risk is theft.

Internal vs. External Audits

There are many similarities and differences between an internal audit and an external audit. Among the similarities are the following:
- Both start with the parish's goals and objectives
- Both conduct testing routines that analyze many transactions

- Both look closely at parish financial procedures and the staff's appreciation of the importance of compliance

- Both look closely at information systems, a principle element of the financial control process

- Both seek to uncover errors that affect the parish's financial accounts

In addition to the fact that the external auditor is independently contracted while the internal auditor is an employee of the organization (although acting independently), the primary difference is that the external auditor is most concerned with financial statements and the financial transactions upon which they are based. They render an opinion as to whether they provide a true representation of the parish's financial position. The internal auditor focuses on the parish's operations, especially regarding risk management and internal controls. Once internal auditors have identified a risk, they advise the parish on executing effective controls and evaluating their effectiveness and efficiency. In other words, while the external auditor is more concerned with the accuracy of the parish's financial statements, the internal auditor is more concerned with its business practices.

Fr. Dave had heard tales of serious embezzlements within the Church, both at the parish and diocesan levels. He was aware of a study[1] that showed that 85 percent of U.S. Catholic dioceses had experienced at least one embezzlement in their parishes within the past few years, and many had experienced more than one, some running to millions of dollars.

He knew of priests and lay staff members who had been sent to prison for embezzling from the church. But he had to believe that members of his parish staff, both paid and volunteer, were above reproach. He had been working closely with these people for the past few months, and he trusted them implicitly. The whole process seemed like a waste of both parish and diocesan staff time. It was an inconvenient interruption to the real work of the church.

Mary had never participated in an internal audit, since the last pastor change had occurred prior to her becoming business manager. Neither she nor Fr. Dave knew what to expect. All they could do was make sure that the financial reports and supporting documentation were in order. Over the next few weeks, Mary spent a good deal of her time preparing for the audit.

The Audit and Report

The auditor arrived as scheduled and spent the next three days poring over the parish's financial reports and aligning them with supporting documentation. Everything seemed to be in order. However, the auditor also spent time interviewing Fr. Dave, Mary, and the chair of the finance council about a variety of parish money handling policies and procedures. He even showed up on Sunday morning to observe the parish's collection counting routine.

Within a month, the auditor's report arrived on Fr. Dave's desk. The auditor had given the parish a satisfactory rating with respect to its financial condition. However, accompanying the report was a series of management letter comments. **Management letter comments** relate to control deficiencies that could result in the inaccurate collection of data for financial reporting or the risk of theft. The

1. Robert West and Charles Zech, "Internal Financial Controls in the U.S. Catholic Church," *Journal of Forensic Accounting* 9 (2008): 142.

control deficiencies are referred to as either significant deficiencies or material weaknesses, depending on the likelihood of errors or fraud passing through the parish's system without detection.

> **Material weaknesses** are deficiencies in internal controls that present the prospect that the organization's financial statements may contain misstatements that can't be detected or prevented. **Significant deficiencies** are not as severe as material weaknesses, but significant enough to warrant attention.

While breathing a sigh of relief that the auditor had found the parish's financial statements were in order, Fr. Dave was nevertheless embarrassed by the critical assessment of the parish's internal financial controls. He met with Mary and the parish finance council and set about the task of addressing the issues raised in the management letter comments.

What are some of the common internal financial control failings that often plague parishes, and which might have appeared in St. Michael's management letters? What are some of the best practices in addressing these issues?

Parish Internal Financial Controls Issues and Actions

Internal financial controls are those processes and procedures, common in the business world, that are used to ensure the proper handling of funds. Besides ensuring that accurate data appear in the parish's financial reports, they are meant to both discourage and detect theft. Unfortunately, the auditor found that St. Michael's processes and procedures were found wanting in a number of ways.

Each of the following issues and the accompanying recommendations might be viewed as controversial by those staff and parishioners affected. Putting strong internal financial controls in place where previously there had been none might elicit the response, "What, you don't trust us?" They might feel that their integrity is being questioned. The proper response by the pastor is, "This is for your and my own protection. If, heaven forbid, there is an irregularity with our parish finances, you and I will be protected from suspicion as long as we have properly implemented strong internal controls."

Establish Policies and Procedures

Since any organization, including a parish, experiences a multitude of transactions in each period, it is important that the organization demonstrates consistency in the way that transactions are recorded in order to get an accurate picture of its finances. The **Financial Accounting Standards Board (FASB)** has developed standards to ensure that transactions are handled in a consistent manner. At a minimum, a parish should be applying these standards. In recent years, most dioceses have established their own standards, consistent with the FASB standards but reflecting their own needs for financial reporting and accumulating data from a number of entities, including parishes, schools, and social service agencies. Frequently these standards are embedded in software that all parishes are recommended (or required) to use. In any event, the parish should have some point of reference for assigning their transactions on a consistent basis.

Action 1: A policy and procedures manual, based on diocesan protocols,
will be established to ensure that similar transactions are handled in similar ways.

Limit the Number of Bank Accounts

It's not unusual in a typical parish for each ministry or organization to want control of their finances. Each will insist they need their own checking account. They don't. If a parish has too many checking accounts it makes it difficult, if not impossible, for the parish leadership to maintain control of finances. This will impact not only the ability of the parish to provide accurate financial information, but will greatly increase the opportunity and the temptation for embezzlement.

> In a classic case, when the Diocese of San Diego declared bankruptcy in 2007 in conjunction with the clergy sexual abuse scandal, it was discovered that the average parish had eight checking accounts. The presiding judge wondered aloud how any parish could effectively control its finances with that many individual checking accounts. The authors have tales of parishes with more than fifty checking accounts, each controlled by a separate parish organization. This is clearly untenable.

In reality, some parish organizations do need their own checking account. A parochial school, for example, needs its own account. A national fraternal organization, like the Knights of Columbus, could justify having its own checking account. But the choir, adult education committee, youth group, and so forth will also argue that they need their own separate checking account. The vast majority of parish organizations could easily get by with simply having individual line items in the parish's statement of accounts, one for revenue and one for expenses. That would allow the parish to control the organization's finances while still providing the opportunity to monitor its budget. This goal can easily be accomplished by following the budget formulation tactics we discussed in earlier chapters. By creating a budget that is built by program area, there is no need for separate accounts because managers can easily access reporting information.

Parish organizations that have been accustomed to controlling their own finances by having their own checking account will surely complain if that privilege is taken away. How should the pastor respond? "This is for your own protection."

Action 2: Ascertain the number of parish bank accounts.
Going forward, limit them to allow greater control and less opportunity for error or wrongdoing.

Limit Authorized Check Signers

Just as it is important that the parish limit the number of checking accounts, it is likewise important to limit the number of authorized check signers. It is very difficult for a parish to control its finances, much less prevent error or wrongdoing, when five, six, seven, or even more have the authority to sign checks.

At the same time, checks in large amounts should require the signatures of two individuals. What constitutes a large amount? It depends on the parish and what routine expenses look like. Perhaps a check for one hundred dollars would be a large amount in one parish, while one-hundred-dollar checks are routine in another. The parish doesn't want to bog staff down getting two signatures on routine checks. In a typical parish, surely a check for $1000 or more would not be routine and should require two signatures.

Action 3: Limit authorized check signers. Checks in large amounts
will require the signatures of two responsible individuals.

Require Supporting Documentation

It is important that all understand that any parish expenditure must be supported by adequate documentation. This is true when dealing with vendors, but it is particularly true for staff and parishioners who have spent their own funds on an item for parish use and now expect to be reimbursed. As we emphasized in chapter 6 when discussing budget execution, a parish expense requisition form should be developed. Procedures for requesting cash advances, reimbursements, and purchase orders need to be established. An expense authorization process that requires receipts or other documentation needs to be in place.

It is critical that the standard be set, with no exceptions: no documentation, no reimbursement.

This could be a delicate policy to implement in a parish that previously had not required documentation for reimbursement. Many parishioners will complain when confronted with this new policy. The pastor's response? "This is for your own protection." Over time, once parishioners have had sufficient opportunity to adjust to the policy, and they see that it is applied to everyone uniformly, any pushback should cease.

Action 4: Disburse funds according to procedures prescribing systematic expense authorization, including adequate supporting documentation as described in chapter 6.

Implement Collection Controls

Many parishes are very cavalier in their handling of the weekend collection funds. It's not unusual to see an usher take the funds after the offertory procession and walk them across the church parking lot by him- or herself and hand them off to the collection counters. Even if the usher is not tempted to skim a few bills from the basket, the opportunity for a mugging and theft in the parking lot is there.

Once the funds have been handed off to the collection counters, there are other internal control issues. Some parishes have only one person counting the collection, sometimes just the pastor, on Sunday afternoon or evening. Other parishes use a regular crew of counters, the same people counting the collection week after week. Both of these approaches offer a high degree of temptation. Many embezzlements have been discovered because a different individual counted the collection, or a different individual joined the collection counting team, and as a result, collection revenues increased significantly that week.

Best practices include the following:

- Immediately after the collection, the funds should be placed in a **tamper-proof (sealable) bag** and logged in. The bag number, date, and Mass time should then be recorded in a control log. At least two ushers sign the control log.

- Either the tamper-proof bag should be placed in a safe or other locked and secure area, or it should be delivered to the collection counters by at least two ushers. If the bag has been placed in a safe, at least two members of the collection counting team should retrieve it.

- The collection counting team should have the following characteristics:

  - At least three individuals on each team

  - At least three teams that rotate

  - No members of a team related to each other by blood or marriage

- The tamper-proof bag is opened in the presence of all collection counting team members.

- After the funds have been counted, they are placed in a safe along with a completed bank deposit form that has been initialed by each member of the collection counting team.

- At least two individuals take the funds to the bank to be deposited, and return with a deposit receipt issued by the bank. The amount on that deposit receipt must match the amount on the deposit form that had been initialed by the collection counting team members.

A similar process should be in place for the collection revenue at other parish events, such as fundraisers.

When these best practices are first introduced, the parishioners involved might feel as though their honesty is being questioned. It should be clearly communicated to all involved that this policy is being implemented to safeguard their integrity. Again, it is for their own protection.

Action 5: Implement the use of tamper-proof bags to hold collections until they are counted. Ensure that more than one individual transports the collection from the church to the collection counting room. Use teams of rotating collection counters. Have more than one individual deposit the collection with the bank.

*Reflection Question: How would you approach a team of collection counters who have been the **only** collection counting team for years to inform them of policy changes without alienating them and other parishioners?*

Segmentation of Duties

In some parishes, one person counts the Sunday collection. The same person deposits the collection funds with the bank and is then responsible for issuing all of the parish's checks. And the same person is then responsible for reconciling the checkbook.

There are no checks and balances when one person performs all of these tasks. This system places too much temptation in their hands. There needs to be **segmentation of duties**. That is, no one person should perform two consecutive functions in the financial chain of events. Where possible, it is even preferable to have a separate person perform each of these tasks. Naturally, in a parish with a small staff, that might not be possible. At a minimum, as noted above, there should be rotating collection counting teams staffed by parish volunteers and more than one person should be involved in depositing the collection. A different person should be charged with reconciling the checking account.

It is not just in the handling of collection funds where the segmentation of duties is important. In fact, it might be even more important, and the temptation to steal even greater, in the case of other parish revenues such as parish fundraisers, which are heavily cash based. This is just another reason why the parish administration should control all revenues, even those raised by individual parish organizations or ministries.

Action 6: Segment the duties associated with the counting, depositing, check writing, and checking account reconciliation for all parish revenues among as many different individuals as possible.

Electronic Giving

The parish has one other tool for reducing the opportunity for theft that hasn't been described in this chapter because it is technically not a means of internal control—electronic giving. Most banks will work with parishes to set up a system whereby parishioner contributions are transferred directly from their bank account to that of the parish, typically at the beginning of the month. This system has numerous advantages:

- Since the funds are contributed at the beginning of the month, before other parishioner bills are paid, it represents "firstfruits," a biblical stewardship standard.

- Many parishioners admit that their weekly contribution depends to a large extent on how much money is in their checking accounts. Most parishioners have more money in their checking accounts early in the month, so they can be more generous in their parish contributions. But by the end of the month, once they've paid off many of their bills, they have less in their checking accounts and are less generous to their parish. By withdrawing the funds at the beginning of the month, parishes are likely to receive larger monthly contributions.

- Many parishioners fail to make up the lost contributions on those weekends when they don't attend Mass in their home parish, for whatever reason. With electronic giving, since the funds are transferred to the parish automatically, they contribute the same amount each month, whether they attend or not. This also helps to smooth out the parish revenue stream, avoiding the large dips in revenue that many parishes experience over the summer.

- Electronic giving is a form of pledging. Studies show that parishioners who pledge to their parish contribute as much as 47 percent more than those who don't.[2]

- Especially among younger parishioners, electronic payment is second nature. They use it to pay their mortgage, car payment, utility bills, and so on. Using electronic giving to contribute to the parish is as routine for them as writing a check is for their parents.

The concept of *giving firstfruits*, as a standard for good stewardship in supporting God's work, can be found in numerous biblical passages. In fact, there are twenty-nine references to it in the Bible:

- "The best of the first fruits of your ground you shall bring to the house of the LORD your God." Exodus 34:26

- "When you have come into the land that the LORD your God is giving you as an inheritance to possess, and you possess it, and settle in it, you shall take some of the first of all the fruit of the ground, which you harvest from the land that the LORD your God is giving you, and you shall put it in a basket and go to the place that the LORD your God will choose as a dwelling for his name." Deuteronomy 26:1–2

- "Honor the LORD with your substance / and with the first fruits of all your produce; / then your barns will be filled with plenty, / and your vats will be bursting with wine." Proverbs 3:9–10

There is one downside to electronic giving to churches. Some pastors are concerned that if people give electronically they will not participate in the offertory collection, a key element of the liturgy. However, there are some ways around this. For example, the envelope companies that serve most Catholic parishes offer envelopes that have an optional box to check that says, "We have contributed electronically." These envelopes can be placed in the collection basket along with envelopes that contain cash or checks.

Electronic giving is a useful theft prevention tool since it removes the middleman. Funds go directly from the parishioner's bank account to the parish's bank account. The issues discussed in this chapter become irrelevant.

2. Robert West and Charles Zech, "Internal Financial Controls in the U.S. Catholic Church," *Journal of Forensic Accounting* 9 (2008): 129–55.

Action 7: Work with a local bank or a parish consulting firm
and offer parishioners the option of electronic giving.

Chapter Summary

The implementation of internal financial controls is a difficult sell to parishes. After all, no one would think that a member of the clergy, a lay staff member, or a parish volunteer would steal from the church. In fact, staff and parishioners involved in the handling of money could well be offended. But employing good financial controls is good stewardship. It ensures parishioners that their financial contributions are valued and protected, and will be used for the purposes for which they had intended. As for the parish staff and volunteers, as was repeated frequently during this chapter, it is for their own protection.

Combining the discussion found in this chapter and that in chapter 6 on budget execution leads to the following:

Top Ten Tips for Budget Execution and Control

1. Develop standard operating procedures.

2. Define and communicate terminology, and provide clear instructions.

3. Clarify roles and responsibilities for financial procedures.

4. Explain to others the importance of internal controls—
   "This is for your own protection."

5. Create templates for common tasks. Use resources already available
   (financial management software, archdiocesan/diocesan policies, etc.).

6. Be patient, change takes time. New policies and processes take
   time for people to adjust.

7. Remember the 3 R's when errors occur: **Reflect** on what occurred, **Review** if/
   what changes are necessary, **Refine** policies and procedures.

8. Ensure receipts and support documentation are included prior
   to disbursing funds.

9. Seek the services of a financial professional when necessary (CPA, auditor, etc.).

10. A simple process is better than no process at all.

In the next chapter, Fr. Dave will learn the tools and techniques of financial analysis.

References

West, Robert, and Charles Zech. "Internal Financial Controls in the U.S. Catholic Church." *Journal of Forensic Accounting* 9 (2008): 129–55.

Zech, Charles E. *Why Catholics Don't Give...And What Can Be Done About It.* Huntington, IN: Our Sunday Visitor Press, 2006.

Zech, Charles E., Mary L. Gautier, Robert J. Miller, and Mary E. Bendyna. *Best Practices of Catholic Pastoral and Finance Councils.* Huntington, IN: Our Sunday Visitor Press, 2010.

Chapter 9

Parish Accounting and Financial Reporting

Chapter 9 Preview

In this chapter, we will help Fr. Dave to do the following:

- Learn principles of accounting
- Review and make accessible key terminology
- Learn the **accounting equation** (assets = liabilities + net assets)
- Understand financial reports
  - Statement of financial position (balance sheet)
  - Statement of financial activities (income statement)
  - Statement of cash flows
- Translate concepts into actions for effective financial management

St. Michael's Parish—Financial Reports Due

After some great weekend ministry, Fr. Dave is back in the office. He reviews his e-mails and receives the following from Mary:

> To: Fr. Dave
> From: Mary
> Date: July 27
> Re: Diocesan Financial Report Request
>
> Hi Fr. Dave,
>
> I'm hard at work. I've been pulling reports from the parish financial management software to make sure we meet the August 15 deadline to submit our annual financial report to the diocese. This report includes all of the financial information from this past fiscal year (July 1–June 30). The report will detail all of the financial aspects of the parish from account balances to the current real estate values of the church and rectory. The packet of information the diocese requires includes the following:
> - Signed letter by the finance council certifying that they have reviewed and approved the financial statements
> - Statement of financial position
> - Statement of financial activities
> - Statement of cash flows
>
> *E-mail continued on next page*

The software will pull all of the needed reports. We just need to make sure that the numbers add up and then send it over to the diocesan business office. I have to be honest, I know that we have been learning new things about parish finances since you arrived, but this is one of those areas I find very confusing. The finance council can help you in terms of what all of these reports mean to us, but I find it overwhelming.

Thanks,
Mary
St. Michael's Business Manager

After reading the e-mail, Fr. Dave starts feeling anxious yet again about his knowledge of parish finances. He knows the finance council can help him understand the reports, but at the same time, he wants to be prepared. He starts growing more and more uncomfortable as he thinks through some initial questions.

"What do these reports represent and why are they important?"

"I see many terms, but I don't know what they mean."

"Do these reports tell me if we are in good or bad financial shape?"

"How do these reports relate to all of the other documents
we have put together?"

Fr. Dave knows that he is not looking for a full-blown accounting course, but he would like the right level of knowledge to grasp the accounting practices at the parish and understand the financial reports. He knows that if he's armed with this expertise, it will help him and his team become stronger managers and even better stewards of parish finances.

Introduction to Accounting

Accounting is often described as the language of business. You could say that Latin is to the Church as accounting is to finance! *Webster's* dictionary defines language as a "systematic means of communicating ideas or feelings by the use of conventionalized signs, sounds, gestures, or marks having understood meanings," and accounting can be defined similarly. Accounting is the systematic means of recording, managing, reporting, and communicating financial actions of an organization. Let's learn the language of accounting so that you are able to understand and translate what you are reading. As a language, it's also good to note that many accounting terms have Latin roots. For example, the Latin translation of the word **debit** means "he owes" and **credit** means "he trusts."

Accounting has a rich history. Its roots are in ancient Mesopotamia, the Roman Empire, and the Catholic Church. Did you know that a key figure in the history of modern accounting was a Franciscan friar, Luca Pacioli (1447–1517)? An Italian mathematician, Pacioli is known throughout the world as the "Father of Accounting and Bookkeeping." His textbook, *Summa de arithmetica, geometria. Proportioni et proportionalita* (Venice, 1494), is the foundational text from which modern accounting comes.[1]

---

1. "Luca Pacioli," *Wikipedia*, https://en.wikipedia.org/wiki/Luca_Pacioli.

Luca Pacioli (1447–1517)

During the Italian Renaissance, Venetian merchants used Pacioli's method of double-entry accounting. Many of the terms, principles, and practices of modern accounting have deep historical roots in this innovative Franciscan friar's publications. Accountants' use of journals, ledgers, assets, liabilities, financial reports including the balance sheet, income statement, and much more, are all credited to Pacioli.

Laws and Regulations

In any language, there are grammar rules, pronunciation guidelines, even a variety of dialects. The same is true in accounting. As we noted in chapter 8, the Financial Accounting Standards Board (FASB) is the governing board that regulates the wide variety of rules and regulations for accounting in the United States. The day-to-day set of accounting practices, standards, and definitions used for accounting are called the **Generally Accepted Accounting Principles (GAAP)**. Certified Public Accountants (CPAs) are required to know these standards as part of their professional certification.

What Is FASB?

"Since 1973, the Financial Accounting Standards Board has been the designated organization in the private sector for establishing standards of financial accounting and reporting. Those standards govern the preparation of financial reports and are officially recognized as authoritative by the Securities and Exchange Commission and the American Institute of Certified Public Accountants. Such standards are essential to the efficient functioning of the economy because investors, creditors, auditors, and others rely on credible, transparent, and comparable financial information."[2]

Along with FASB rules and regulations and GAAP standards, parishes must also abide by the laws and regulations related to the federal tax code and exempt status as executed by the IRS. From a Catholic Church governance perspective, the **Code of Canon Law**, "Book V: The Temporal Goods of the Church," contains the canons regarding the acquisition, retention, administration, and alienation of temporal goods.[3] Most archdioceses/dioceses also produce a set of policies and procedures related to recording parish financial transactions.

There are many books on understanding and implementing accounting principles and practices. Our goal in this chapter is to provide you with the right level of detail to understand accounting principles and concepts as well as learn the questions you should ask when reviewing information. For those looking for even more detailed information on accounting, there is a list of recommended references for further study at the end of this chapter.

2. "Facts About FASB," Financial Accounting Standards Board, http://www.fasb.org/facts/.

3. "Book V: The Temporal Goods of the Church," in the Code of Canon Law, canons 1254–1310.

Accounting Methods

This brings us to the methods in which parishes record financial transactions. There are two primary methods of recording financial transactions: cash basis and accrual basis.

Cash Basis

In c**ash basis** accounting, **revenues** are recorded when money is actually received and expenses are recorded when money is actually paid. Therefore, from an accounting perspective, regardless of when you expect money to come in or when you know a bill is to be paid, you record the transaction when you deposit a donor's check or make a payment for goods or services.

Accrual Basis

In **accrual basis** accounting, revenue is recorded when it is earned and expenses are recorded when they have been incurred. Hence, using this method, revenues and expenses are recorded regardless of when the cash is received or disbursed.

St. Michael's—Renting the Tent

In May, Fr. Dave and Mary signed a contract with a local vendor, JJ Rentals, to lease a tent for the parish picnic in August. Even though Fr. Dave signed the contract in May, if the parish is using a cash basis, the expense would not appear in the ledger until the check is cut and mailed to JJ Rentals for payment. Alternately, using an accrual basis, the rental fee would be recorded in the accounts payable section of the ledger when the contract is signed because the parish knows they have committed to making this payment. Reports prepared for the finance council will look different depending on the accounting method used. The accrual basis will offer a more accurate financial position because it will show that there is an outstanding bill that has been incurred but not yet paid.

Modified Cash Basis

There is a hybrid model that can be used called the **modified cash basis** for recording transactions. This method uses a cash basis to record income as it is deposited and expenses when they are paid; however, when financial reports are pulled for a given period, they also include outstanding *accounts receivable* and *accounts payable*.

St. Michael's—Accounting Method

Continuing our example above, if St. Michael's uses a modified cash basis for their accounting method, we can solve the issue of cash on hand seeming overinflated (knowing a big bill is coming due) by offsetting this amount in the accounts payable section of the report.

Making Financial Terminology Accessible

Chart of Accounts

Think of the **chart of accounts (COA)** as a master code that the parish will use to keep track of all of the accounts and categories in the financial operation of the parish. The COA is the systematic structure that categorizes all financial accounts and tracks money coming in and money going out from the parish. Hierarchical in format, the structure is a coding system for the variety of account types, programs, and the variety of income and spending categories. A series of digits make up the structure for understanding the type, level, and detailed information related to an account or budget line item. Often, the archdiocese/diocese will publish a standard chart of accounts to be used for all parishes. For example, the first-level digit might be a 1 to indicate assets, 2 to indicate liabilities, and so on. The digits that follow provide more granular data. An example is displayed in figure 9-1.

Figure 9-1
Sample chart of accounts coding system

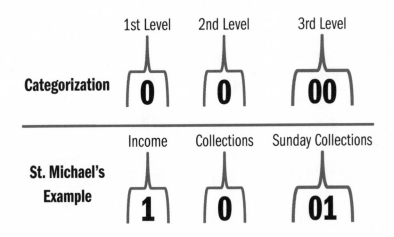

Ledgers and Journals

If you keep a personal journal where you record significant events in your life, think of the series of journals and ledgers as the place where you record financial "events" in the life of the parish. This format allows every transaction in the parish to be recorded. As part of the parish financial management software, you might have a general ledger, cash receipts, accounts receivable journal, check writing system, and payroll disbursement system.

The Accounting Equation

In financial transaction recording, you will come across the term **double-entry accounting**. In double-entry accounting, every transaction is recorded as a debit or credit in ledgers and journals to ensure that both sides of "the accounting equation" remain in balance. The accounting equation is this:

Assets = Liabilities + Net Assets

Let's review each component of this equation.

Assets

In short, *assets* are what the parish owns. Parish assets include cash available from the parish checking and savings accounts, receivables such as pledges, things owned by the parish such as computer equipment, and other fixed assets like the parish buildings.

Liabilities

Liabilities are amounts owed to others. Current liabilities for the parish may include payment for the archdiocesan/diocesan assessment and staff salaries and benefits. Noncurrent liabilities are items like mortgage and loan payments.

Net Assets

Once you account for assets and liabilities, the remaining balance (funds available) are **net assets.** In business, the terms *retained earnings* or *owner's equity* are used instead of *net assets*. Whereas businesses use resources to generate profits for shareholders, the parish uses these resources (net assets) to further its mission.

Three categories of net assets exist for parishes: unrestricted, temporarily restricted, and permanently restricted. **Unrestricted assets** are resources available for any purpose after all money is received and bills paid. **Temporarily restricted assets** are donations that are limited by donor-imposed stipulations that either expire by the passage of time or are fulfilled by actions of the parish. **Permanently restricted assets** are contributions that have been made for a specific and designated purpose and must only be used for those purposes.[4] Now that we have a basic vocabulary for key terms in financial management, let's turn to the subject of financial reporting.

Understanding Financial Statements

A key concept to understanding financial statements is to remember that one statement on its own does not fully represent the entire financial landscape of the parish. Reviewed *together*, financial statements can help answer a variety of questions and provide a more accurate representation of the parish finances.

In our workshops, we see church managers struggle to read, interpret, and understand financial statements. To help them understand these concepts, we like to have them relate this topic to their personal finances, and then it seems to make more sense.

If we say, "Tell me about your personal financial situation and how things are going." you might say, "I have about $5,000 in my checking account and about $50,000 saved." Would this be the most *comprehensive* representation of your finances for a given period? Probably not. A more accurate representation would include a discussion and report on *all* areas of your financial life with specificity. You might say,

> I have $5,556 in my checking account and $52,030 saved. I own a house where I plan to retire, and I have paid about half of my thirty-year fixed mortgage. The parish reimburses me for some expenses like gas that I use for parish-related activities. I personally pay eighty dollars monthly for my cell phone and thirty dollars for a gym membership. I also have two accounts that I am unable to use until I retire, a 401K with $125,000 and a Roth IRA with $30,000.

Now this report would provide a more accurate and full representation of your finances. Let's carry the example further into the language of financial reporting so you can make the connections.

---

4. Code of Canon Law, canon 1267 §3; cf. also c. 1284 §2, 3°–4°.

- **Assets**—Begin the report with money that can quickly be turned into cash (liquid accounts). This would include the money from your checking and saving accounts. The current value of your house is considered a noncurrent asset because selling the house would take time to turn into cash, since it would involve marketing and selling the house to a willing buyer.

- **Liabilities**—Some of your current liabilities include monthly payments for cell phone and gym membership. Long-term liabilities would include your mortgage balance, since it will not be entirely paid within one year.

- **Restricted funds**—Resources you have that are tied up until retirement, like a 401K or Roth IRA.

As you can see, translating daily life into these types of terms helps. After we discussed additional details about our personal finances, we had a fuller picture of our financial situation. The same is true with the financial reports we discuss that follow.

Let's now discuss each one that makes up the typical financial reporting package.

Statement of Financial Position

The statement of financial position details the assets *owned* and liabilities *owed* by the parish on a particular date that the statement is reported. Note that we said "on a particular date." Think of the statement of financial position as a *picture* of the parish finances on a particular date. In the other reports, we will review the account for a specified period, like watching a video. So the statement of the financial position is a snapshot in time. The other reports provide more of a running narrative.

You'll also hear the statement of financial position called the *balance sheet*. This term can help you remember how this report works, because when there is a change in assets or liabilities or net assets, there must be an equal change in another category of assets or liabilities or net assets.

Financial statements list assets and liabilities in order of liquidity. **Liquidity** is simply defined as how quickly an asset can be turned into cash or when a liability will be paid. To remember the concept of liquidity, think of liquids to remember the definition. Say you ask for a drink. You could be given a glass of water or a glass of ice that will eventually melt into water. What's the difference? You can drink the water right away. If you only have a glass of ice, you have to wait until it melts.

Let's translate the analogy into parish management. If you have cash from Sunday collections in a checking account (current asset—water) that you can pull out of the bank at any time, that's considered very liquid. If you have to advertise, contract, and sell church land (fixed asset—ice) it will take longer to turn into cash and is therefore less liquid. Table 9-1 displays a sample statement of financial position for St. Michael's.

Table 9-1
St. Michael's statement of financial position
As of June 30

	As of June 30, 20XX
Assets	
Current Assets	
Checking Account	$110,726
Deposits with Diocese	425,000
Savings Account	50,000
Other Investments	-
Total Current Assets	**585,726**
Fixed Assets	
Church	980,000
Rectory	355,000
Equipment/Furniture	149,500
Total Fixed Assets	**1,484,500**
Total Assets	**2,070,226**
Liabilities and Net Assets	
Liabilities	
Accounts Payable	17,000
Due to Diocese	35,350
Other Liabilities	12,000
Loans Payable	-
Total Liabilities	**64,350**
Net Assets	
Unrestricted	1,815,876
Temporarily Restricted	175,000
Permanently Restricted	15,000
Total Net Assets	**2,005,876**
Total Liabilities & Net Assets	**$2,070,226**

Statement of Activities

The parish's **statement of activities** displays the current revenue, expenses, and the difference between the two as change in net assets. You'll remember from when we crafted the budget that when more money comes into the parish (revenues) then goes out (expenses), we have a surplus of funds. If this is reversed, we have a deficit. In the for-profit world, you'll often hear this report referred to as the *income statement*. This distinction is made because the goal of commercial entities is to increase shareholder value, whereas the nonprofit organization's goal is to use resources to further its mission. If there is an increase in net assets, the resources are returned back into the organization to further the mission. In the for-profit world, an increase in equity is returned to shareholders as dividends or invested in the business to generate more profits.

Unlike the statement of financial position, which is a snapshot of parish finances as of a particular date, the statement of activities will be pulled for a given *period*. For most parish organizations, the fiscal year is July 1–June 30, although this report can be pulled from the parish financial management software at any time. Think of this report as watching a video that includes all the transactions over a period of time, in comparison to the statement of financial position that is comparable to a still photograph.

Table 9-2
St. Michael's statement of activities
July 1–June 30

	Unrestricted	Temporarily Restricted	Permanently Restricted	Total
Revenues				
Collections	$707,000			$707,000
Donations	1,100	15,400		16,500
Programs	7,500			7,500
Other Income	11,254		2,746	14,000
Total Revenues	726,854	15,400	2,746	745,000
Expenses				
Personnel	264,121			264,121
Diocesan Assessment	70,700			70,700
Administrative/Office	89,145			89,145
Liturgical/Sacramental	45,500			45,500
Programs	58,000			58,000
Plant and Facilities	115,700			115,700
Total Expenses	643,166	-	-	643,166
Increase (Decrease) in Net Assets	$83,688	$15,400	$2,746	101,834
Net Assets at the Beginning of the Year	1,732,188	159,600	12,254	1,904,042
Net Assets at the End of the Year	$1,815,876	$175,000	$15,000	$2,005,876

Statement of Cash Flows

The **statement of cash flows** displays how the parish has used the money that has come in, the money that has been spent, and any investments or other financial transactions that have been made. The main goal of this report is to display cash inflows and outflows.

Unlike the statement of activities that reports all money in and out for operational expenses, the cash flows statement also shows any additional sources of inflows or outflows that may not appear on the activities statement. There are three components to the statement of cash flows: cash flow from operations, cash flow from investing activities, and cash flow from financing activities.

Cash Flow from Operations

The key word here is *operations*! This portion of the report lists inflows or outflows to *operate* the parish day to day. Included will be incoming money from sources like Sunday collections, stole fees, and bulletin advertising money. Money that is spent on things like office supplies and utilities will be on the outflows portion of this report.

Cash Flow from Investment Activities

Cash flow from investment activities includes money spent on major equipment purchases or other assets or money that was received from the sale of these assets. For example, if St. Michael's boiler breaks down and they purchase a new boiler but sell the old boiler's parts to a contractor, you would have an inflow of cash from the sale of the old parts to the contractor and an outflow that would include the payment for the new boiler.

Cash Flow from Financing Activities

Cash inflow from financing activities includes any money received from borrowing or other financing activities that the parish has engaged in. If St. Michael's decides to renovate the parish hall, they may decide to take out a loan for construction costs. The money that St. Michael's receives from the bank is an inflow. Any debt repayment on the loan is an outflow.

Table 9-3
St. Michael's statement of cash flows
Year ending June 30

	Year Ending June 30
Cash Flow from Operating Activities	
Increase in net assets	$101,834
Adjustments to reconcile changes in net assets to cash from operating activities	
Depreciation	27,532
Decrease in prepaid assets	1,100
Increase in accounts payable	3,150
Decrease in accrued expenses	-8,500
Net cash provided from operating activities	$125,116
Cash Flow from Investments	
Purchase of equipment	-9,500
Net cash used for investment	-9,500
Cash Flow from Financing	
Payments on notes payable	$0
Net cash provided to financing	$0
Sum of Net Increases in Cash for Year	**$115,616**
Beginning Cash Balance	**$470,110**
Ending Cash Balance	**$585,726**

The statement of financial position reports the value of assets owned, liabilities owed, and status of net assets on a specific date (e.g., June 30). The statement of activities and statement of cash flows provide additional details on operational income, expenses, changes to net assets and cash flows from operating, investing, and financing activities for a period of time (e.g., July 1–June 30). Taken together, the financial statements, supported by other parish documents (e.g., budget and variance reports), paint a comprehensive picture of the parish's financial situation.

Financial Records

As we conclude our discussion on financial statements, we also want to cover the importance of records retention. Records retention is crucial for a number of purposes, from legal requirements by the IRS, to archdiocesan/diocesan reporting and accountability, and for the present and future financial management at the parish.[5] As we have already stated in the budget formulation, execution, and control chapters, comparison of financial information from previous periods, whether weeks, months, or years, will provide a wealth of data and insights for current and future generations of parish management staff.

Financial Management Assistance

Select Technology to Meet Parish Needs

Targeted parish financial management software has evolved well over the last decade. From accounting to human resources to stewardship tracking, software is continually being improved and enhanced to meet the needs of a thriving parish. As we have noted, many archdiocese/diocese require specific parish management software be used. Take the time to understand the key features of the software you have. Become educated on the variety of functions the software offers as well as the variety of reports that can be pulled.

If specific software is not required, we recommend that parishes brainstorm key requirements so that the selection of software serves the needs of the parish. Technology is only as good as the needs that it serves. Take time to think through your requirements.

Provided that a staff member is able to enter transactions into the software, the reports described previously are not difficult to access. Just remember to ensure that proper internal controls are established (described in the previous chapter) and that those responsible for financial reporting are educated on how these reports can be read.

Top Ten Actions for a New Parish Leader/Manager

We recognize that the task of leading any parish budgeting and financial management process can seem daunting. However, this guidebook's purpose is to synthesize key concepts so that you have the best methods and techniques to lead the parish in the present and beyond. With that in mind, before we go any further, we want to offer you ten actions you can take to understand the financial landscape you are addressing at your parish.

1. Review archdiocesan/diocesan budget and financial policies (chapter 1).

2. Understand the current budget process and identify any gaps relating to collaboration and budget transparency (chapters 2 and 3).

---

5. For more information, see United States Conference of Catholic Bishops, *Diocesan Financial Management* (Washington, DC: Committee on Budget and Finance, 2009), XVI–1, XVI–2.

3. Learn about what methods are used to formulate the budget and identify any gaps relating to budget guidance and techniques deployed (chapters 4 and 5).

4. Learn about current budget execution policies and procedures (chapter 6).

5. Employ the QUEST model to review financial information. Seek a current variance report that includes the actual income received and money spent compared to budgeted/projected income and spending (chapter 7).

6. Determine when the last financial audit was conducted and decide if one is needed. If an audit was conducted, review all management letter comments (chapter 8).

7. Assess the current status of internal controls established and identify any gaps (chapter 8).

8. Learn about the financial management software that the parish has in place and its reporting capabilities. Review the COA and understand all current accounts listed in the name of the parish (chapter 9).

9. Identify all parish assets, including fixed assets (facilities, etc.) and any other capital assets (technology, etc.) that the church possesses (chapter 9).

10. Review the current and previous two years of financial statements: statement of financial position, statement of activities, and statement of cash flows. Compare and contrast the reports (chapter 9).

Chapter Summary

We recognize that the variety of terms, standards, and recording methods of accounting and financial reporting is challenging. However, we also firmly believe that by learning the fundamental concepts and language of financial management, as you have done in this chapter, you're empowered with the right level of knowledge to take the next step and go from insight to action. As you review financial statements, keep the following in mind:

- The statement of financial position enables you to review assets, liabilities, and net assets as of a *specific date*. The accounting equation is helpful: Assets = Liabilities + Net Assets. This report is also known as the balance sheet because changes on either side of the equation impact an equal change on the other side.

- The statement of activities provides an overview of revenues minus expenses for a given *period* and shows the change in net assets.

- The change in net assets is the first line item of the statement of cash flows. This report displays the various changes of operating, investing, and financing cash flows at the *conclusion of the period* under review.

Remember that the goal of these financial reports is to have them complement one another so that a full picture on parish finances emerges. If you find yourself unable to answer a question or feel ill-equipped to address a specific situation, always remember that you can reach out to others for support. Many archdioceses/dioceses have great financial resources available to you, including staff, to assist you. Use the members of your parish finance council to discuss questions, policies, procedures, and brainstorm strategies. Finally, there are a variety of financial management professionals like CPAs and other financial experts ready and willing to assist you.

Like many concepts we have discussed in this book, understanding and applying these principles and techniques takes practice. Similar to learning a language, you'll grow more and more comfortable with the vocabulary, and as time passes, gain fluency in this remarkable language.

In chapter 10, we leverage all of the budget and financial management concepts we have learned so far and teach you practical tools to implement that improve decision making and bring additional efficiency and effectiveness to parish operations.

References

Blazek, Jody. *Nonprofit Financial Planning Made Easy*. Hoboken, NJ: John Wiley & Sons, 2008.

Finkler, Steven A. *Finance and Accounting for Nonfinancial Managers*. New York: Aspen Publishers, 2003.

——. *Financial Management for Public, Health, and Not-for-Profit Organizations*. New York: The Robert F. Wagner Graduate School of Public Service, New York University, 1998.

United States Conference of Catholic Bishops. *Diocesan Financial Management*. Washington, DC: Committee on Budget and Finance, 2009.

Section III

Financial Management

Analysis, Insight, and Action

Chapter 10

Informed Decision Making

Analysis, Insight, and Action

Chapter 10 Preview

In this chapter, we help Fr. Dave to do the following:

- Learn how financial analysis can help inform decision making
- Discuss common action steps to conduct any analysis
- Learn methods, terminology, and outcomes of the following analytical tools:
  - Benefit/cost analysis
  - Breakeven analysis
  - Activity-based resourcing
- Understand how analysis can bring insight and action

St. Michael's Parish—Decisions, Decisions!

Growing more and more confident in his approach to budgeting and financial management, Fr. Dave wants to take his learning to the next level and utilize this information to help inform him on other decisions he confronts as the parish leader.

He has the following decisions on his mind:

"Do we buy or lease a new copier?"

The copy machine continues to break down and has become a problem. It has been on the fritz for at least a year, and it is frustrating for anyone to use it, whether it's the staff or parishioners planning an event. Fr. Dave would like to consider two options: (1) purchase a new copier or (2) lease a copier and pay a monthly fee.

"How can we break even for an event that was not budgeted?"

The unemployment rate in the area surrounding St. Michael's has increased over the last few years. St. Michael's social justice committee has put together a proposal to host a community job fair. The goal of the job fair is to bring employers and job seekers together. Unfortunately, this event was not planned in the budget and there are costs associated with it.

"How can I help address resourcing (time, money, or people) challenges?"

In her one-on-one meetings with Fr. Dave, Mary has repeatedly been telling him, "I am so overwhelmed and I don't even know where my time goes. From managing the finances, checking e-mails, and my work with the staff, time just evaporates." There is too much to do and too little time to do everything.

Fr. Dave is willing to learn new tools and techniques to help him make better decisions, but he gets frustrated when reading books on the topic because they are either too confusing or too business focused and not applicable to parish life.

Ready...Set Goal...Go

We want to help Fr. Dave learn easy-to-use financial analysis tools and techniques to assist him in making decisions. This can be extremely useful to Fr. Dave on a number of levels. The benefits include the following:

- A systematic methodology to analyze, assess, and determine the next course of action for a given challenge or opportunity
- Tools and techniques that can help assess trade-offs
- Breaking down complex problems into solution-oriented results

Don't let the concepts below intimidate you. Like everything we have discussed previously, try some of them out, start simple, and practice. Some methods will work better than others, depending on what you are trying to accomplish and what techniques work better in your organization's culture.

We will use a series of challenges faced by St. Michael's to illustrate the methods we describe. To practice as we teach, open your favorite spreadsheet software, follow us through the techniques, and try these methods yourself.

Whether you use parish financial software, pen and paper, or any other technology, once you learn the method, you'll not only be able to conduct these analyses on your own, but you'll be able to explain them to others. A helpful hint as you read: don't focus on the particular problems that we are trying to solve, but focus on how the outcomes of each method can serve you in making decisions.

Action Steps

Below are four steps to remember in every analysis you conduct:

Step 1: Understand the goal(s)

Step 2: Collect data and information

Step 3: Conduct analysis

Step 4: Make recommendations

Step 1: Understand the Goal(s)

Notice the word we added in the title of this section to the typical marathon running formula—*Goal!* As we will discuss in the text that follows, this is *the* critical component in conducting any of the methods we describe. Once you have determined your goal, you will be able to determine which technique(s) will work the best.

Each technique described has a set of objectives and can produce a variety of outcomes. These are not one-size-fits-all solutions. However, we can't stress enough how important it is to be clear about the goal you are trying to achieve with each analysis.

In our experience, we have seen some of these techniques used to validate something that has already been decided. This causes much frustration on the part of the team and other stakeholders. Leaders might wrongly think that no one knows their strategy. However, more often than not, the people involved are not fooled. The team will either work to delegitimize the process or simply refrain from participating altogether. The solution to this challenge is to be clear about the goal. Identifying and clarifying the goal is the first step to every technique listed.

Step 2: Collect Data and Information

Data collection is the step in which you will pull together relevant information that will help you to conduct analyses. As we will describe, different types of data may be needed to meet your goal and the outcome you are hoping to achieve. The type of information you might collect includes the following:

- Demographic data
- Historical financial data
- Survey results
- Benchmark data from research organizations (i.e., The Center for Applied Research in the Apostolate)[1] or other professional or academic organizations.

Step 3: Conduct Analysis

In this step, you will review the goal, consolidate the data, and bring the elements together in a format that can help you weigh your options. Once you establish and bring clarity to the goal, seek all relevant data. This step may end up being the easiest part of the entire process! As you will see, the methods laid out are not overly complex when you are clear about your goal and have data and information at your fingertips.

Step 4: Make Recommendations

Based on the previous three steps, the outcome of your analysis will provide you with the ability to make informed recommendations or decisions. You can present results of your analysis in a variety of formats from simple (i.e., e-mail your findings) to a full-blown report with a table of contents, executive summary, and visuals. As we will discover, depending on what and to whom you are trying to communicate, your decision will help you choose the format.

There are a wide variety of analyses that can be conducted, but we want to illustrate three that we believe can be very helpful in parish decision making.

- Benefit/cost analysis
- Breakeven analysis
- Activity-based resourcing

1. See http://cara.georgetown.edu.

Benefit/Cost Analysis

Benefit/cost analysis (BCA) is a systematic approach that compares and contrasts the benefits and costs associated with alternative options. Familiar terms associated with this technique are cost/benefit analysis (CBA) or alternatives analysis (AA). We like the acronym BCA because it will help you remember the formula for calculating the **benefit/cost ratio (BCR)**. When you understand an investment's benefits (B) and divide (/) by the investment's costs (C), the results help you understand the investment's return on investment.

For our purposes, we will define *investment* as anything that will require a significant outlay of resources (time, money, or people). Whether the investment is money to purchase a capital asset like a new church building, or the time and effort it will take to create or expand a parish program, BCA can help inform your decision. Factors that can help you determine whether to use a BCA include the following:

- **Large investment of resources**—Whether the resource is time, money, or people, BCA can be helpful when a decision requires a sizable outlay of any of these items. We recognize that the concepts of "large" or "sizeable" relating to resources are subjective but that's okay. As we have mentioned in other areas of this book, you can always rightsize these processes to fit your needs.

- **Multiple stakeholders impacted**—If there are multiple stakeholders impacted by a decision (e.g., staff, parishioners, local community, etc.), the analysis can help identify and communicate the pros, cons, and the impact the decision will have on others.

- **Need for justification**—By systematically cataloguing the variety of benefits and costs, the trade-offs between choices become more apparent and offer you an outline for justifying a decision.

Along with reflecting on the factors listed above, you may also consider using BCA for a variety of decision types:

- **Go/No:** Do we *go forward* or do we *decide not to go forward* for a major purchase or project?
  - Example: Should we renovate the parish hall or use the resources for other purposes like expanding our current programs?

- **Lease/Buy:** Should we *lease* or *buy* a product or service?
  - Example: Should we lease or buy a new copy machine?

- **Hire/Current:** As a variation on the above question, do we *hire* a contractor/vendor to meet a specific service need or do we use *current staff*?
  - Example: Should we hire a snow removal service or purchase a plow that maintenance personnel can use when it snows? Do we hire landscapers/lawn care or have the maintenance staff perform this task?

- **Type/Level:** What *level* (platinum, standard, basic version) of a product or service should we buy?
  - Example: What type of boiler model should we buy (high, middle, basic)?

To conduct a BCA, gather information for each option, create a list of all qualitative and quantitative benefits and weigh these against the costs to help you come to a decision.

Conducting a BCA

We will break the process for conducting a BCA into four steps:

1. Determine alternatives

2. Estimate benefits

3. Estimate costs

4. Analyze and recommend

1. Determine Alternatives

Alternatives are the options that you are considering for the analysis. Begin by brainstorming two to four viable options. To determine viability, ask yourself this question: "If we decide to go with option A, B, C, and so on, can we actually do it or is it impractical?" If an alternative is not viable, there is no need to create a paper exercise just because it seems like a good idea. If you are stuck trying to decide on options, remember that you can always use the status quo, if viable. That is, if you do nothing, what are the benefits and costs?

St. Michael's—Determine Alternatives

As we learned at the beginning of the chapter, the copy machine continues to break down and has become a problem. The lease on the current copy machine is up in two months and the team has decided to review options. They decide they want to try out BCA to determine the best course of action. The parish developed a comprehensive list of needs and requirements (color, scanning, fax, etc.). The team brainstormed and researched alternative options and determined that there are two options that they would like to consider:

Option 1: Purchase copier

- Parish *purchases* a copier for $5,500.
- Copier is *owned* by the parish (capital asset) and will be in use as long as the copier works.
- The parish is *responsible* for all costs associated with the copier including all *maintenance*, *supplies* (toner, paper), and *repairs*.

Option 2: Lease copier

- Parish signs a five-year agreement with a *monthly lease* payment of $179.
- The leasing contract *includes annual maintenance and emergency repairs.*
- The parish is *responsible* for *supplies* (ink, paper) but receives a *discount* on these items if purchased through the leasing company.
- Parish has a monthly *copy allotment* of two thousand pages. If the parish exceeds the monthly allotment, the parish is charged a one cent fee for any additional copies.

Now that we have the options we are considering, the next step in the process is to estimate the benefits associated with each option.

---

2. Estimate Benefits

Benefits can be categorized in a number of ways, but consider two primary modes—quantitative and qualitative. **Quantitative benefits** are benefits received that can be valued or measured in some numerical or monetary amount. Examples may include money saved from an investment, cost avoided as the result of a decision, increase in net assets, or so on. **Qualitative benefits** include improvements, enhancements, or additional value that are received that do not necessarily have monetary value but improve, enhance, or bring additional value to the parish in other ways. Let's now go further into reviewing these two types of benefits.

Quantitative Benefits

In the context of parish life, quantitative benefits can make people nervous. The argument is that the goal of a parish is not to return profits to shareholders but to exist as a community of faith dedicated to fulfilling a mission. Converting benefits into numerical or monetary results is not always the first priority of the parish. However, understanding the monetary impact of a decision is important. There are ranges of quantitative benefits, also referred to as tangible benefits, that can result from a decision. Let's look at two common quantitative benefits in the context of parish life.

Cost Savings

Cost savings occur when decisions are made that result in reduced spending on an established budgeted category. Another way to think about cost savings is to answer the question, "How much *less* will the parish need to spend on a given category that has been previously budgeted or spent?" The difference between the previous amount and the new amount is the cost savings. This money is now available for other purposes.

For example, let's say a daughter graduates from college. Her parents tell her that she will now be responsible for her own car insurance and take her off their policy. The parents no longer pay for something that they have always covered. The difference between their previous cost of insurance and their new cost of insurance is considered cost savings. That money is now available for other purposes.

At St. Michael's, the parish may decide that they will e-mail the annual financial report instead of mailing the report to every registered family. The parish previously spent $637 for postage (1,300 families x $0.49 per stamp). As a result of the decision to e-mail the report, the parish will receive cost savings of $637. This amount of money that was previously budgeted for stamps is now available for other purposes.

Cost Avoidance

Cost avoidance answers the question, "How much will the parish *save in the future*?" Cost avoidance refers to reductions that *cause future spending to fall*, but not below the level of current spending. For example, at St. Michael's, the financial report was always printed in black and white. This year, Fr. Dave wants to add color and visuals to the report and proposes going to Sophia's Copy Company (SCC) to have the report printed. However, as a result of the decision to e-mail the report, the parish will not incur the additional printing expense at SCC and therefore the cost is avoided.

Reflection Question:
As we discussed, the parish previously printed and mailed the
financial report to all parishioners. Given the recent decision to e-mail the report, St. Michael's
no longer has to use paper and toner that they previously budgeted for this purpose. Is this
an example of cost savings or cost avoidance?

Continuing the example of the college graduate daughter from above, say she decides to buy a new car. She narrows her choice between two options. As she is reviewing the costs and benefits, she notes that one car requires regular fuel and the other requires premium fuel. Even though her parents paid for her insurance, she always paid for her own gas and she will have to pay for fuel *regardless of her choice*. Because we are discussing benefits, if she chooses the car that requires regular fuel, the difference between the price of premium and regular fuel can be considered cost avoidance.

Notice that we made clear that we are discussing benefits. You may be thinking, "You could also look at this factor in reverse. If the daughter decides to go with the car that requires premium fuel, she will have to pay more for fuel and therefore the cost of operating her vehicle will increase. Should we also include fuel as a negative on the cost side of the BCA if she chooses the premium-fuel car?"

The answer depends! We want to caution you against *double counting* both a benefit and a cost for the same factor of equal value. In this case, you choose whether to include fuel as a cost avoidance benefit of the regular-fuel car, or as a negative for the premium-fuel car because it will cost more to operate. *The key is that you cannot account for the same factor of equal value on both sides of the BCA.* Otherwise the regular-fuel car option gets twice the value for avoidance of additional fuel costs (benefit) and receives value because it is less expensive to operate (costs). Alternatively, the premium-fuel car is negatively impacted for the same factor on both sides of the equation. By being cautious against double counting benefits and costs, your analysis will not give an option an unfair advantage.

Once the benefits have been brainstormed, you must now estimate the impact of these benefits. To estimate and project potential benefits, you can use the budget preparation skills learned in chapters 4 and 5 to create your forecasted benefit.

St. Michael's—Estimate Quantitative Benefits

St. Michael's has brainstormed the following quantitative benefits as it relates to their option to buy or lease the copier.

Table 10-1
Buy/lease quantitative factors

Quantitative Benefits	Buy New	Lease
Utility Cost Reduction	New copier is more energy efficient than current copier, resulting in an 8% reduction in annual utility costs, approximately $1,000.	Leased copier is also more energy efficient than current copier, resulting in an 8% reduction in annual utility costs, approximately $1,000.
External Printing (Fliers/Ads/Pamphlets)	New copier will remove need for many items that the current copier cannot produce, including fliers, ads, and pamphlets.	With a concern for overage charges, parish will be reluctant to use the lease copier for production of fliers, ads, and pamphlets and will continue the practice of using a printing service.
Discounted Supplies/Ink/Paper	Supplies discount does not apply.	Vendor has agreed to provide a discount of supplies of 12%.

You'll note that the utility cost reduction is the same for both options. When we calculate and analyze the information (following), you will see that the reduction in utility costs is included for both options. This benefit will not provide an advantage to either of these two options because they are equal. However, the reason we want to include this type of benefit is to make sure the analysis is comprehensive. If we were to add a third alternative to the BCA to purchase a used copier from another parish, the older copier may not have the utility reduction benefit and therefore the benefit would not be included for that option.

Qualitative Benefits

Qualitative benefits, also referred to as intangible benefits, include benefits that may not convert to monetary benefits but bring improvements in other areas. These types of benefits include improvements in team effectiveness, staff and parishioner morale, or community services. Below are some common areas that can be considered when brainstorming qualitative benefits.

- **Strategic benefits:** Benefits that move a parish closer to achieving its mission, vision, or strategic priorities.

- **Direct user benefits:** Benefits directly realized by users or multiple user groups. Users will vary based on the type of initiative assessed. Users may include, but are not limited to, parish staff, parishioners, or in the case of a school, teachers and students.

- **Social (nondirect user/public) benefits:** Benefits achieved by a broader community and no single direct user. For example, the placement of a prayer garden will bring a wide range of benefits not only to the parish but to the larger community. The community at large includes neighbors and employees who work close by and others who seek a quiet spot to meditate.

- **Operational benefits:** Benefits focused around results related to processes, procedures, and actions that create efficiency or effectiveness for an organization. Examples of operational benefits include improvements in quality, speed, and reliability for operational tasks or responsibilities. Benefits may also include improvements in human capital, asset management (facilities, information technology), and the acquisition of goods and services.

Additional qualitative benefits include the following:

- *Administrative*—Will the amounts of administrative work increase or decrease?
- *Redundancy*—Will the investment reduce redundant tasks?
- *Morale*—Will the investment improve the working environment?
- *Flexibility*—Will the staff be able to respond to a greater number and variety of requests?
- *Simplicity*—Will operations be simplified or made more complex?
- *Consistency*—Will the quality of the services become more consistent?
- *Speed*—Will you be able to respond more quickly to requests?
- *Quality*—Will the investment include better parish services?

St. Michael's—Estimate Qualitative Benefits

The team has brainstormed the following qualitative benefits as it relates to their option to buy or lease the copier.

Table 10-2
Buy/lease qualitative factors

Qualitative Factors	Buy New	Lease
Ownership	The parish owns the copier (capital asset) and will be able to use it as long as it functions.	The parish is not committed to owning a large capital asset, and the commitment does not extend beyond the five-year agreement.
Breakdowns and Repairs	In the case of a breakdown, parish will have to find a company to come fix the printer.	As part of the leasing agreement, if machine breaks down, repair service is provided.
Staff Effectiveness	Team will be more efficient because the current copier is frustrating when it does not work.	Team will be more efficient because the current copier is frustrating when it does not work.
Maintenance	Parish staff is responsible for scheduling maintenance.	Leasing company schedules maintenance appointments.
Supply Purchases	Staff may need to shop around for discounted supplies (toner, paper, and so on).	Discounted supplies are included in the contract; parish staff can order supplies directly from vendor.
Tracking Overages	No overage charges apply because parish owns copier. Staff will not be required to track number of copies.	Contract stipulates overage charges. Parish staff will need to track number of copies made.
External Printing (Fliers/Ads/Pamphlets)	New copier will remove need for many items that the current copier cannot produce, including fliers, ads, and pamphlets.	With a concern for overage charges, parish will be reluctant to use leased copier for production of fliers, ads, and pamphlets and will continue practice of using a printing service. Staff time will be necessary for staff to leave facilities and go to external printing company.

3. Estimate Costs

After you have created a list of benefits, turn to the costs associated for each alternative. As a best practice when making any financial decision, include an investment's full lifecycle costs. **Lifecycle costs** are the estimated cost elements for a particular alternative over the time period corresponding to the life of the investment. These estimates include direct and indirect initial costs, plus any periodic or continuing costs of operation and maintenance.

Typically, the way costs are laid out is by cost elements. A **cost element** is a category of cost (or type of cost). There are many ways of categorizing costs. Options include costs categorized by project phase (planning, maintenance), by the types of items or services procured (hardware, software, system architecture and design), or both. Usually, there are major cost elements and sub-elements that fall underneath them.

Use the same procedure that you used to estimate benefits to determine costs associated with a decision. Note that we include *year 0* to indicate an up-front cost; for subsequent years, we assume that the cost will occur at the end of that period. For example, if the copier is purchased for $5,500, this would be a cost linked to year 0. Alternatively, a lease payment would be made throughout the year and typically at the end of each month; therefore, we place this cost in the columns for years 1–5.

St. Michael's—Estimate Costs

The results of the staff's research on cost elements and considerations are summarized in table 10-3.

Table 10-3
Copier buy/lease costs

Costs	Buy New	Lease
Payment	Up-front charge for purchase—$5,500	Payment over time of $179 per month Year 1 = $2,150 and the same amount for years 2–5.
Emergency Service Calls and Repairs	Emergency services not included and is an additional charge.	As part of agreement, vendor will arrive at customer's office on average in less than four hours from the time the service call is placed.
Maintenance	Additional maintenance contract needed for new copier.	Maintenance of copier is a component of the lease agreement.

While addressing cost factors, you will also note some nuances. Note that we did not include the cost of time spent by staff to make copies. This is not included in our analysis because this cost does not vary across options. Whether we buy or lease, this factor does not change and can be excluded.

Be sure to document any assumptions you make regarding all components of this analysis. For example, Fr. Dave and team may want to note that they considered the cost of time spent on making copies but determined this would not be included because this cost does not vary by option.

4. Calculate and Analyze

Now that we have collected information on our alternatives, documented assumptions, and estimated both benefits and costs, we can consolidate the information and determine the trade-offs between the options.

Table 10-4
Buy new copier—benefits and costs

Buy New—Benefits	Year 0	Year 1	Year 2	Year 3	Year 4	Year 5	Totals
Utility Cost Reduction		$1,000	$1,000	$1,000	$1,000	$1,000	$5,000
Remove Need for External Printing (Fliers/Ads/Pamphlets)		$2,000	$2,000	$2,000	$2,000	$2,000	$10,000
Total Benefits		$3,000	$3,000	$3,000	$3,000	$3,000	$15,000
Buy New—Costs	Year 0	1	2	3	4	5	Totals
Initial Investment	$5,500						$5,500
Maintenance Contract		$550	$550	$550	$550	$550	$2,750
Emergency Services		$1,000	$1,000	$1,000	$1,000	$1,000	$5,000
Total Costs	$5,500	$1,550	$1,550	$1,550	$1,550	$1,550	$13,250

Financial Management: Analysis, Insight, and Action

Table 10-5
Lease copier—benefits and costs

Buy New—Benefits	Year 0	Year 1	Year 2	Year 3	Year 4	Year 5	Totals
Utility Cost Reduction		$1,000	$1,000	$1,000	$1,000	$1,000	$5,000
Discounted Supplies/Ink/Paper		$2,000	$2,000	$2,000	$2,000	$2,000	$10,000
Remove Need for Emergency Calls during Copier Breakdown		$1,000	$1,000	$1,000	$1,000	$1,000	$5,000
Total Benefits		**$4,000**	**$4,000**	**$4,000**	**$4,000**	**$4,000**	**$20,000**
Buy New—Costs	Year 0	1	2	3	4	5	Totals
Initial Investment	$0						$0
Annual Lease Payment		$2,150	$2,150	$2,150	$2,150	$2,150	$10,750
Total Costs	**$0**	**$2,150**	**$2,150**	**$2,150**	**$2,150**	**$2,150**	**$10,750**

Time Value of Money

The time value of money principle is based on the premise *a dollar today is worth more than a dollar tomorrow*. Why? If you have money today, you can do something with it. Maybe you will want to put the money into an interest-bearing savings account or invest in the stock market, or you may decide to stuff the money under your mattress for safekeeping. The challenge is that tomorrow, the next day, and all the days that follow are more uncertain than the known value of the money today.

Will inflation cause your money to be worth less or more in the future? How will fluctuations in the stock market affect your investments? What happens if your cash is stolen? These are common concerns in the world of money.

Imagine that you have fifty dollars in your pocket right now. The fifty dollars in your pocket is valuable to you because you can use it, right now. On the other hand, it is uncertain whether you will have fifty dollars tomorrow and how much it will be worth. Tomorrow you might need to spend the money on a major car repair or on medication because you become ill.

We use the term *opportunity cost* to describe what is given up in terms of value as a result of the decision you are making. When you make a decision, you trade-off value between your choice and the next best option. Conventional wisdom suggests that if you choose to put your money into a savings account, the risk of losing your money is far less than in the more volatile and less predictable stock market. However, the opportunity cost (what you give up) is the possibility of receiving a higher return on investment, if you take the next best option (stock market). The time value of money principle helps ensure that the values being considered are measured in a comparable way.

Therefore, in order to ensure that we can account for things like inflation or compound interest that occur when you invest money, we want to calculate the present or future value of money that we have estimated.

The equation for calculating the present value:

Equation 10-1
Calculating Present Value

$$\text{Present Value (PV)} = \text{Value} \div [(1 + \text{Discount Rate}) \wedge \text{Time Period}]$$
$$PV = \text{Value} \div [(1 + r) \wedge t]$$

Calculators and spreadsheet programs allow you to do this very quickly with just a few data elements. Let's explore each element of the formula so that if you want to, you can easily calculate this on your own as well.

Present value (PV) = The value of future receipts or payments discounted to the present. Remember, the time value of money is the principle that a dollar today is more valuable than the same amount in the future.

Value = The estimated receipt or payment for the given time period.

Discount rate (r) = The interest rate used in time value of money calculation.

Raised to the 'nth power (^) = The symbol ^ is used to indicate the number that must be multiplied times itself (t) to equal a given value.

Time period (t) = The time period (e.g., months or years) that you are multiplying for the given value. If you are calculating the present value at the end of the first year, t will equal 1 because the discount period has occurred one time. At the end of the second year, t will equal 2 because the discount period is compounded twice, and so forth.

Looking at table 10-6 below, we include how to calculate the present value of expected benefits for the decision between buying a new copier or leasing.

Table 10-6
Sample formulas for calculating the present value of benefits

Row/Column	A	B	C	D	E
1	Alternative 1	Year 1	Year 2	Year 3	Totals
2	Benefit X	$ Amount	$ Amount	$ Amount	Total Benefit X
3	Benefit Z	$ Amount	$ Amount	$ Amount	Total Benefit Z
4	**Total**	**Sum B2:B3**	**Sum C2:C3**	**Sum D2:D3**	**Sum E2:E3**
5	**Present Value Calculations**				
6	Alternative 1	Year 1	Year 2	Year 3	Totals
7	Benefit X	B2 Value ÷ (1 + r) ^ t	C2 Value ÷ (1 + r) ^ t	D2 Value ÷ (1 + r) ^ t	Sum B7:D7
8	Benefit Z	B3 Value ÷ (1 + r) ^ t	C3 Value ÷ (1 + r) ^ t	D3 Value ÷ (1 + r) ^ t	Sum B8:D8
9	**Total PV**	**Year 1 PV (Sum B7:B8)**	**Year 2 PV (Sum C7:C8)**	**Year 3 (Sum C7:C8)**	**Year 4 Sum (E7:E8)**

St. Michael's Example

Below, we display the details of calculating the present value of the utility cost reduction. We will use a discount rate of 2 percent to account for inflation.

Equation 10-2
St. Michael's Example

Benefit: Utility Cost Reduction of $1,000 per Year for 5 Years

Present Value (PV) = Value ÷ [(1 + Discount Rate) ^ Time Period]

Year 1 Utility Cost Reduction Benefit—$1,000

$$PV = \$1,000 \div [(1 + 2\%) \wedge \text{Year } 1]$$
$$= \$1,000 \div [(1.02) \wedge 1]$$
$$= \$1,000 \div 1.02$$
$$= \$980 \ ^{2.}$$

Equation 10-2 continued on next page

Equation 10-2 continued

Year 2 Utility Cost Reduction Benefit—$1,000

$$PV = \$1,000 \div [(1 + 2\%) \wedge \text{Year 2}]$$
$$= \$1,000 \div [(1.02) \wedge 2]$$
$$= \$1,000 \div 1.04$$
$$= \$961$$

Year 3 Utility Cost Reduction Benefit—$1,000

$$PV = \$1,000 \div [(1 + 2\%) \wedge \text{Year 3}]$$
$$= \$1,000 \div [(1.02) \wedge 3]$$
$$= \$1,000 \div 1.06$$
$$= \$942$$

Year 4 Utility Cost Reduction Benefit—$1,000

$$PV = \$1,000 \div [(1 + 2\%) \wedge \text{Year 4}]$$
$$= \$1,000 \div [(1.02) \wedge 4]$$
$$= \$1,000 \div 1.08$$
$$= \$924$$

Year 5 Utility Cost Reduction Benefit—$1,000

$$PV = \$1,000 \div [(1 + 2\%) \wedge \text{Year 5}]$$
$$= \$1,000 \div [(1.02) \wedge 5]$$
$$= \$1,000 \div 1.10$$
$$= \$906$$

Now that Fr. Dave understands the present value equation in action for the reduction in utility costs, he can calculate the present value of all benefits and costs for both options.

Table 10-7
Option 1: Buy new copier—benefits
Summary of benefit present value calculations

	Year					
Buy New—Benefits	**1**	**2**	**3**	**4**	**5**	**Totals**
Utility Cost Reduction	$1,000	$1,000	$1,000	$1,000	$1,000	$5,000
Remove Need for External Printing (Fliers/Ads/Pamphlets)	$2,000	$2,000	$2,000	$2,000	$2,000	$10,000
Estimated Benefits	**$3,000**	**$3,000**	**$3,000**	**$3,000**	**$3,000**	**$15,000**
Present Value						
Utility Cost Reduction	$980	$961	$942	$924	$906	$4,713
Remove Need for External Printing (Fliers/Ads/Pamphlets)	$1,961	$1,922	$1,885	$1,848	$1,811	$9,427
PV Benefits	**$2,941**	**$2,884**	**$2,827**	**$2,772**	**$2,717**	**$14,140**

2. Note that numbers are rounded off.

Table 10-8
Option 1: Buy new copier—costs
Summary of costs present value calculations

Buy New-Costs	Year 0	Year 1	Year 2	Year 3	Year 4	Year 5	Totals
Initial Investment	$5,500						$5,500
Maintenance Contract		$550	$550	$550	$550	$550	$2,750
Emergency Services		$1,000	$1,000	$1,000	$1,000	$1,000	$5,000
Totals	**$5,500**	**$1,550**	**$1,550**	**$1,550**	**$1,550**	**$1,550**	**$13,250**
Present Value							
Initial Investment	$5,500						$5,500
Maintenance Contract		$539	$529	$518	$508	$498	$2,592
Emergency Services		$980	$961	$942	$924	$906	$4,713
PV Costs	**$5,500**	**$1,520**	**$1,490**	**$1,461**	**$1,432**	**$1,404**	**$12,805**

Table 10-9
Option 2: Lease copier—benefits
Summary of present value calculations

Lease Benefits	Year 1	Year 2	Year 3	Year 4	Year 5	Totals
Utility Cost Reduction	$1,000	$1,000	$1,000	$1,000	$1,000	$5,000
Discounted Supplies/Ink/Paper	$2,000	$2,000	$2,000	$2,000	$2,000	$10,000
Remove Need for Emergency Calls during Copier Breakdown	$1,000	$1,000	$1,000	$1,000	$1,000	$5,000
Estimated Benefits	**$4,000**	**$4,000**	**$4,000**	**$4,000**	**$4,000**	**$20,000**
Present Value						
Utility Cost Reduction	$980	$961	$942	$924	$906	$4,713
Discounted Supplies/Ink/Paper	$1,961	$1,922	$1,885	$1,848	$1,811	$9,427
Remove Need for Emergency Calls during Copier Breakdown	$980	$961	$942	$924	$906	$4,713
PV Benefits	**$3,922**	**$3,845**	**$3,769**	**$3,695**	**$3,623**	**$18,854**

Table 10-10
Option 2: Lease copier—costs
Summary of present value calculations

Lease Costs	Year						
	0	1	2	3	4	5	Totals
Initial Investment	$0						$0
Annual Lease Payment		$2,150	$2,150	$2,150	$2,150	$2,150	$10,750
Totals	$0	$2,150	$2,150	$2,150	$2,150	$2,150	$10,750
Present Value							
Initial Investment	$0						$0
Annual Lease Payment		$2,108	$2,067	$2,026	$1,986	$1,947	$10,134
PV Costs	$0	$2,108	$2,067	$2,026	$1,986	$1,947	$10,134

Benefit/Cost Ratio

Now that we have the present value of both the benefits and costs for each option, we can summarize the data and calculate the benefit/cost ratio.

Equation 10-3
Benefit/Cost Ratio

Benefit/Cost Ratio (BCR) = Present Value (PV) Benefits ÷ PV Costs

New Copier BCR = PV Benefits ÷ PV Costs
= $14,140 ÷ $12,805
= 1.10

Lease Copier BCR = PV Benefits ÷ PV Costs
= $18,854 ÷ $10,134
= 1.86

Table 10-11
Copier buy/lease benefit cost ratio summary

		Buy New	Lease
Benefits	Value	$15,000	$20,000
	PV Benefits	$14,140	$18,854
Costs	Value	$13,250	$10,750
	PV Costs	$12,805	$10,134
	Benefit Cost Ratio	1.10	1.86

To interpret the result from the benefit/cost ratio calculation, a good rule of thumb is that the higher the ratio the better the return on investment. A quick tip that can help you understand your results is to add a $ to the ratio, then fill in the blanks to the following statement.

For every $1 of spending on the option to _____, we receive a benefit/cost ratio of _____.

St Michael's—Results

1. For every $1 of spending on the option to *buy a new copier*, we receive a benefit/ cost ratio of *$1.10*.

2. For every $1 of spending on the option to *lease a new copier*, we receive a benefit/ cost ratio of *$1.86*.

Of the two options explored, which one gives St. Michael's a better return on investment from a quantitative perspective? The conclusion that we can draw from a benefit to cost ratio indicates that dollar for dollar, the lease is the better of the two options. However, before making the final decision, Fr. Dave and team must also analyze the qualitative factors.

Qualitative Factor Analysis

Qualitative factors are a key component of any BCA, but are an especially important area for a non-profit organization, like a parish, where the ultimate goal is not returning profits but achieving mission goals and objectives. Hence, developing a simple process to evaluate qualitative factors is extremely important and beneficial as you make trade-offs between options. When analyzing qualitative factors as a component of BCA, we recommend using a method that scores each factor on the extent of the *impact* on the achievement of parish mission, vision, and goals.

A simple format that you can use to calculate the impact a qualitative factor has on fulfilling parish mission and goals is to score individual factors by option. Create and define a simple numeric scale and score each factor. When you complete the scoring, add up the total for each option. The score can then be used as an additional way to evaluate the alternative options. Together with the benefit/cost ratio, you can review both qualitative and quantitative factors and make a decision.

You may also consider having multiple people score the factors and then facilitate a discussion when reviewing the results. We recognize that scoring qualitative factors is subjective. However, do not let this discourage you from involving others. In fact, encourage individuals to offer their perspectives. As we have stated numerous times in this book, individuals that are directly impacted by a decision are more likely to buy into the outcome if they are involved in a transparent process. However, you must say how the results/feedback will be used when making the decision.

St. Michael's—Qualitative Factor Scoring

Instead of having each member of the parish staff score the factors on their own, Fr. Dave led a collaborative meeting with the staff to discuss each factor and used the following rating scale.

Rating Scale

- Enter a score of 5 if the factor has a *positive impact* on fulfilling parish goals.
- Enter a score of 3 if the factor has *neither/both* positive or negative impact on fulfilling parish goals.
- Enter a score of 1 if the factor has a *negative impact* on fulfilling parish goals.

The parish staff was in agreement on how the factors impacted the fulfillment of parish mission. On the next page is a summary of the results discussed at the meeting.

Table 10-12
St. Michael's copier decision
Summary of qualitative factor scoring

Qualitative Factors	BUY NEW	Score	LEASE	Score
Ownership	The parish owns the copier (capital asset) and will be able to use it as long as it functions.	3	The parish is not committed to owning a large capital asset and the commitment does not extend beyond the five-year agreement.	3
Breakdowns and Repairs	In the case of a breakdown, parish will have to find someone to fix the printer.	1	As part of the leasing agreement, if machine breaks down, service is provided.	5
Staff Effectiveness	Team will be more efficient because current copier is frustrating when it does not work.	5	Team will be more efficient because current copier is frustrating when it does not work.	5
Maintenance	Parish staff is responsible for scheduling maintenance. The staff will be required to keep track of when maintenance appointments are required.	1	No need for parish staff to worry about when annual maintenance will occur. Leasing company schedules maintenance appointments.	5
Supply Purchases	Staff may need to shop around for discounted supplies.	1	Discounted supplies are already included in the contract; parish staff can order supplies directly from vendor.	5
Tracking Overages	No overage charges apply because parish owns copier. Staff will not be required to record number of copies made.	5	Contract stipulates overage charges. Parish staff will need to record number of copies made.	1
External Printing (Fliers/Ads/Pamphlets)	New copier will remove need for many items that the current copier cannot produce including fliers, ads, and pamphlets.	5	Because of overage charges, parish will be reluctant to use leased copier for production of fliers, ads, and pamphlets and will continue using a printing service. Staff time will be necessary to go to external printing company.	1
	Score Total	**21**	**Score Total**	**25**

Fr. Dave and team conclude from the results of the scoring exercise that the option to lease the copier outweighs the qualitative factors to buy the copier. Along with the positive results of the benefit/cost ratio, Fr. Dave makes the decision to go forward with the lease option.

BCA Takeaways

When two or more options exist for a decision, BCA is a systematic way to outline the quantitative and qualitative factors under consideration. BCA is never intended as a black-and-white exercise that results in clear winners and losers, although the analysis is powerful at clarifying decision outcomes. By calculating the benefit/cost ratio and evaluating qualitative factors, you can weigh options on the investment's impact to the organization from different viewpoints. Never underestimate the power that human experience can add to the decision-making process. People are a key resource when undertaking any analysis and can complement the information that is being evaluated.

Breakeven Analysis

Breakeven analysis is a great tool for decisions that involve determining at what point a program, project, or event will pay for itself.

The statement below can help you formulate the factors you will be considering. Fill in the blanks to determine what you are trying to accomplish, list your assumptions, and conduct the analysis.

> *At what level does _____ allow the _____ to become financially self-sufficient?*

The answer to this question can be determined using the following steps:

> Step 1: Document *assumptions*
>
> Step 2: Determine *fixed costs*
>
> Step 3: Determine *variable costs*
>
> Step 4: Calculate *breakeven amount*

St. Michael's—Job Fair

We can use the community job fair proposal, discussed at the beginning of the chapter, to walk through the steps of a breakeven analysis. There is a budget line item for the social justice committee, but this proposal was not part of the budget request. Fr. Dave likes the idea, but as we learned in chapter 7, resources are limited. The program can only go forward if it is self-sufficient.

A member of the committee, who has been talking with local employers, tells the committee, "Employers are willing to pay a fee to be at the job fair to help cover the costs." To break even on this event, what fee should St. Michael's charge and how many employers be recruited? We can fill in the blanks of our opening breakeven analysis statement:

> *At what level does [our fee and the number of employers we recruit] allow the [community job fair] to become financially self-sufficient?*

1. Document Assumptions

As we discussed in chapter 2, assumptions are your expectations, predictions, and projections to help you outline and document your expectations. You can return to these assumptions often to determine whether your expectations are correct or incorrect and then make adjustments as necessary.

Based on research conducted by the committee, the following information was compiled for the event:

- Room rental = $500 for a room that holds up to 375 people
- Lunch for employers = $17 per attendee
- Assume that each employer will bring no more than two people to the job fair
- Advertising and copy costs will not exceed $150
- Table rentals = $10 per table rented, capacity of thirty total tables

Table 10-13
Job fair budget and assumptions

Category	$	Assumptions
Income		
Employer Fees	$40–$70	The committee believes that they can charge employers a fee between $40–$70. This analysis will help them determine how much to charge and the number of employers needed to break-even.
Expenses		
Room Rental	$500	Room can accommodate a total of 375 attendees.
Advertising	$150	Advertising budget will be no more than $150.
Table Rentals	$10	$10 per table per employer.
Lunch for Employers	$8.50	Lunch is $8.50 per individual. Each employer will bring 2 people ($17).

Because you have read previous chapters of this book, you know that this budget can be reviewed and adjusted from a number of different perspectives. For example, questions that may emerge include the following:

- Must we provide lunch to the employers?
- Can we reduce our advertising costs and just do word-of-mouth advertising?
- Can we find a location that will donate use of a room for this event?

These are all relevant questions. However, for our purposes, let's agree that these options have been explored. The committee has decided to go forward with their plan to rent a room and provide lunch. Let's move to the next step and determine fixed costs associated with the event.

2. Determine Fixed Costs

Fixed costs are expenses that do not change as volume increases or decreases for goods produced or distributed or services offered.[3] Examples of fixed costs for the parish may include staff salaries and benefits or debt repayment for the parish hall. Whether one hundred or one thousand people use the parish hall, the monthly mortgage payment does not change; therefore the costs are considered fixed.

St. Michael's Job Fair—Fixed Costs

What are the *fixed cost(s)* for the job fair?

Room rental—The room rental is an example of a fixed cost because the room fee is the same regardless of the number of employers/employees that attend. We know from our assumptions that the room can accommodate no more than 375 people. Whether we have ten people or 375 people, the room fee remains the same.

Advertising—The committee has determined that the total dollars allocated for advertising will not change, regardless of the number of attendees. The parish wants as many attendees as possible but has put a limit on this budget.

---

3. Refer back to chapter 5 for more information.

3. Determine Variable Costs

In contrast to fixed costs, variable costs are those expenses that directly change as a result of the variation in the volume of goods and services produced or delivered. In parishes, variable costs may include the costs of providing textbooks for students in religious education or sacramental supplies. These costs have a *direct relationship* to the goods distributed (e.g., bulletins), services (e.g., parish nurse), program (e.g., religious education), or event (e.g., job fair).

St. Michael's Job Fair—Variable Costs

What are the *variable costs and factors* for the job fair?

- *Lunch for employers*—The amount depends upon the number of employers that attend the event.

- *Table rentals*—The hotel is willing to provide tables for employers at a cost of ten dollars per table. This is a direct cost of the event because it depends upon the actual number of employers that sign up.

4. Calculate Breakeven Amount

Now that we have documented our assumptions and determined our fixed and variable costs, we can calculate the breakeven amount.

Equation 10-4
Calculate the Breakeven Amount

The equation for calculating the breakeven amount is this:

Breakeven Amount = Fixed Costs ÷ (Price/Fee/Quantity - Variable Costs)

Translating the equation for the job fair program, the calculation will be the following:

Breakeven Amount = Job Fair Fixed Costs ÷ (Employer Fee – Variable Costs per Attendee)

As displayed in table 10-14, we have already determined that the total of fixed costs for the event is $650.

Table 10-14
Job fair fixed costs

Fixed Costs	
Room Rental	$500
Advertisement Costs	$150
Fixed Costs	*$650*

We can also calculate the variable costs per employer attendee by adding all variable costs. This totals $27 per employer, as shown in Table 10-15 on the following page.

Table 10-15
Job fair variable costs

Variable Costs	
Lunch ($8.50 x 2)	$17
Table Rentals	$10
Variable Costs per Employer	**$27**

Next, we can calculate the breakeven amount by putting this all together into our formula.

Equation 10-5
Calculating the Breakeven Amount

Breakeven Amount = Fixed Costs ÷ (Fee – Variable Costs Attendee)

Option 1: $40 Fee

= Fixed Costs ÷ (Fee - Variable Costs Attendee)

= $650 ÷ ($40 - $27)

= $650 ÷ $13

= 50 Employers

Option 2: $50 Fee

= Fixed Costs ÷ (Fee - Variable Costs Attendee)

= $650 ÷ ($50 - $27)

= $650 ÷ $23

= 28 Employers

Option 3: $60 Fee

= Fixed Costs ÷ (Fee - Variable Costs Attendee)

= $650 ÷ ($60 - $27)

= $650 ÷ $33

= 20 Employers

Option 4: $70 Fee

= Fixed Costs ÷ (Fee - Variable Costs Attendee)

= $650 ÷ ($70 - $27)

= $650 ÷ $43

= 15 Employers

Table 10-16
Job fair breakeven amount summary

	Option 1	Option 2	Option 3	Option 4
Total Fixed Costs	**$650**	**$650**	**$650**	**$650**
Fee Charged per Employer	$40	$50	$60	$70
Variable Costs per Employer	$27	$27	$27	$27
Fee - Variable Costs	**$13**	**$23**	**$33**	**$43**
Quantity of Employers Needed to Breakeven	50	28	20	15

Now that the information is consolidated, we can make an informed decision. What conclusions can you draw from the data? There is no one right answer to this question, but there are key points to notice.

Breakeven Analysis Results

We know from our assumptions that the room can only hold thirty tables, so we can immediately eliminate option 1 because having fifty employers is not feasible. The more nuanced part of the decision is to determine what fee and what number of employers will meet our needs.

An additional way to look at this data is to calculate a ratio between the numbers of employers and the number of expected attendees. We want to ensure that we don't have too many or too few employers, given the crowd we expect. If we have two hundred job seekers, what is the number of employers to job seekers?

Employers to job seekers ratio calculation

Option 1—Eliminated because we do not have enough room for 50 employers

Option 2—200 job seekers ÷ 28 employers = 7 job seekers per employer

Option 3—200 job seekers ÷ 20 employers = 10 job seekers per employer

Option 4—200 job seekers ÷ 15 employers = 13 job seekers per employer

Option 3 is likely to meet St. Michael's needs for a few reasons. Recruiting twenty employers seems more achievable than recruiting twenty-eight employers, due to the size of the event. The sixty dollar entry fee, which includes lunch and the opportunity to meet a number of potential hires, is a good investment for the employers. Assuming ten job seekers per employer also seems reasonable.

For this type of event, maximizing the number of employers that can fit into the room may not bring the best result. Therefore, you can see how human judgment is an important factor and should not be underestimated in decision making. When we add the employer-to-job-seeker ratio, option 3 becomes the most practical for our goals.

You may have come up with a different answer and that is absolutely acceptable. Like each of the analyses we have presented, the key is not a "right" answer, but one that is justifiable, reasonable, and makes the most sense given the various assumptions and constraints.

Breakeven Analysis Takeaways

Similar to other types of decision analyses, when trade-offs exist between options, breakeven analysis helps you to outline and organize information for alternative options. Breakeven analysis will help you determine the level, quantity, or volume at which point a program, project, or event pays for itself. By reviewing and documenting assumptions, determining the associated fixed and variable costs, place the factors into the equation **Breakeven Amount = Fixed Costs ÷ (Price/Fee/Quantity - Variable Costs)** and summarize the results. As you face questions about financial self-sufficiency or stability of programs or services, breakeven analysis is a great tool to have at your disposal.

Activity-Based Resourcing

Activity-based resourcing (ABR) is a variation on the business analysis tool called activity-based costing. The reason we like *resourcing* instead of *costing* is that this analysis can go beyond costs to other types of resources like time and people. ABR helps you determine the amount of resources necessary to undertake or complete an activity such as programs, projects, specific tasks, or services.

Begin the analysis by defining the activity you want to evaluate and the resource(s) you are assessing. Examples may include the following:

- **Time:** The number of hours spent on administrative (indirect) and program-specific (direct) activities associated with a given role, project, program, and so on.
- **Money:** The expense it takes to complete an activity.
- **People:** The number of people it takes to complete an activity.

Determine Direct/Indirect Resources

The same technique used in the breakeven analysis will also be used here to assess resources. The only difference is that, depending on the analysis, you will identify the direct and indirect **resources** (not only costs) for a given task. This means that along with actual expenses associated with a given program, you can also use other metrics in the analysis.

Identify the direct and indirect costs for a given activity. For example, if we were to determine the direct and indirect resources for administering the sacramental life of the parish, what would be considered direct and indirect costs?

Examples of direct resources related to this activity include the costs of sacramental supplies or the amount of time the pastor spends leading liturgies, preaching, or administering sacraments. On the other hand, indirect costs are the resources used for the broader administration of the parish and other activities. For example, if the pastor leads a parish staff meeting, it is an indirect cost because the meeting may involve a discussion about the liturgies but also include other topics like the faith formation and music programs.

St. Michael's—Mary Is Overwhelmed

Let's return to the example of Mary being overwhelmed in her role as business manager. The first step in conducting this analysis is to set expectations with Mary. As you can imagine, conducting an ABR might make a staff member defensive. They may feel that you are conducting the analysis to micromanage or review their performance because something is wrong. Discussing this with anyone involved in an ABR will be important to ensure this does not happen.

1. Collect Data and Log Information

A good way to start the analysis is by creating a simple log for Mary to document/track her time over a given period. Whether you have Mary complete the log for a few weeks or months depends on how extensive the analysis is to be. We recommend a two- or three-week period to begin with. This will not seem overwhelming, and you will get the required information to conduct the analysis.

There are a number of technological applications that can be used to track time, and these can make this process extremely efficient. Mary can simply enter the tasks that she completes for a given thirty minutes. Below in table 10-17 is a sample log that can be used. Two key columns are needed: *time period* and *task*.

Table 10-17
Sample ABR log

Time	Tasks				
	Day 1	Day 2	Day 3	Day 4	Day 5
9:00					
9:15					
9:30					
9:45					
10:00					
10:15					
10:30					
10:45					
11:00					
11:15					
11:30					
11:45					
12:00					

Mary listed the following key tasks she performs each week:

- Financial transactions
- Financial reporting
- E-mail/phone calls
- Staff management
- Program management
- Parishioner services

She will then log the amount of time she spends on a given task in the log. The listing of associated tasks/responsibilities/activities should be as specific as possible. To the extent possible, try not to have tasks overlap. For example, instead of a task listed as "e-mail," ask what purpose the e-mail was for. Is Mary dealing with a parishioner issue or discussing a financial report with Fr. Dave? E-mail, phone calls, and meetings can be tough to catalog because they can be so general. The granularity of the categories will change depending on your goal.

2. Analyze and Summarize

Once you have collected the data, link the direct and indirect resources to the activity you are evaluating. Add up the hours spent for the various tasks for a given time period and determine the percentage of time spent on each task. On the next page are the results from Mary's log.

Table 10-18
Summary of Mary's activities

Activity	Amount of Time Spent	% of Time
Financial Transactions	15	38%
Financial Reporting	4	10%
E-mail/Phone Calls	13	33%
Staff Management	3	8%
Program Management	2	5%
Parishioner Services	3	8%
Total Time	**40**	**100%** [4]

As displayed in figure 10-1, it may also be helpful to visualize this data in a pie chart or bar graph.

Figure 10-1
Activity summary pie chart

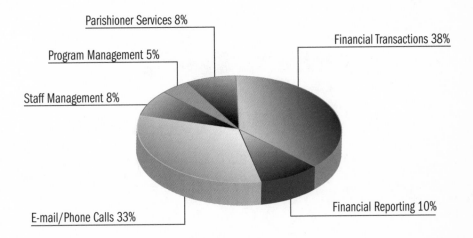

At this point, you may be finished with the analysis. With the percentage of time spent on each task, Fr. Dave and Mary now have the information needed to determine if the various percentages align with her roles and responsibilities. For example, Mary may be spending so much time entering financial transactions that she neglects managing programs or parishioner services that may require more attention.

To take the analysis further, calculate the costs (direct and indirect) associated with each activity. Keep the example simple: calculate Mary's weekly salary and then divide the percentage of time it takes to complete a task by the weekly salary. The result is the estimated weekly costs it takes Mary to complete each task.

Mary's salary: $45,000 ÷ 52 weeks = $865 per week

---

4. Numbers in Tables 10-18 and 10-19 have been rounded.

Table 10–19
Summary of ABR cost results

Activity	% of Time per week	Weekly Costs
Financial Transactions	38%	$325
Financial Reporting	10%	$87
E-mail/Phone Calls	33%	$281
Staff Management	8%	$65
Program Management	5%	$43
Parishioner Services	8%	$65
Weekly Time/Salary	**100%**	**$865**

Figure 10–2
ABR cost results—bar graph

For each activity, we now have the general cost per week associated with the activity Mary completes.

Based on this analysis, Mary realizes that she spends significant time on e-mail/phone calls and logging financial transactions. Whether this is good or bad depends on the goal of the analysis. In this case, Mary may be spending too much time responding to e-mails and phone calls, rather than completing higher-value tasks like parishioner services or program management. Could Edith, the parish secretary, help Mary log transactions, and free Mary for other tasks? These types of questions can be answered when you conduct this type of analysis.

Activity-Based Resourcing Analysis Takeaways

In order to maximize an individual or organization's greatest potential, use ABR to identify and assess the resources (time, money, people) required to achieve goals. Link direct and indirect resources to the activity(s) being evaluated, collect data and information through a tracking mechanism(s), and analyze and summarize the material to inform decision making. Whether the evaluation surrounds roles, responsibilities, or tasks, the results bring a level of awareness and insight that may not otherwise be obtained.

Chapter Summary

Financial analysis brings you a variety of tools and techniques to assist you in the decision-making process. Some key points to remember as you work through any analysis:

- Understand clearly your goals and hoped-for outcomes prior to undertaking any analysis.
- Conduct analysis with a spirit of transparency and collaboration. Ensure that the goals and objectives are clearly communicated so that those involved understand how the results will inform decision making.
- No single method is perfect, but you can obtain powerful insights through decision-making analysis methods.
- Solutions to numerical equations are not always enough to make decisions. Personal (and organizational) experiences and history must be considered as part of any analysis.
- Translate analysis outcomes and conclusions into actionable results.

Benefit cost analysis, breakeven analysis, and activity-based resourcing are fantastic tools at your disposal to systemically collect, analyze, and take action on the variety of decisions you face at the parish. The analyses discussed in this chapter are one more set of tools to inform you on your journey to connect resources and priorities to achieve parish mission, vision, and goals.

Reference

Phillips, Jack J., and Patricia Pulliam Phillips. *Show Me the Money: How to Determine ROI in People, Projects, and Programs*. San Francisco: Berrett-Koehler Publishers, Inc., 2007.

Chapter 11

Fundraising and Capital Campaigns

Chapter 11 Preview

In this chapter, we help Fr. Dave to do the following:

- Understand that fundraising should be a spiritual activity and is a vital component of his ministry as a pastor
- Learn about some of the underlying concepts of fundraising, such as the 20-80 Rule and the 3-1 Rule
- Recognize that although he is expected to lead the capital campaign, he is not in it alone. He has guidance from a campaign consultant and from the parish campaign planning committee that he will appoint
- Understand the specific steps involved in a capital campaign, including
  - Creating a case statement
  - Conducting a feasibility study
  - Identifying a prospect list
  - Soliciting contributions
  - Monitoring the campaign
  - Expressing gratitude
- Acknowledge that a successful campaign should be built on a foundation of stewardship

St. Michael's Parish—The Capital Campaign

The moment that Fr. Dave had dreaded most since he first learned of his appointment to St. Michael's has finally arrived. It was time to initiate the capital campaign to raise the funds to finance renovations to the parish hall. The estimated cost of the project was $1 million. The architectural plans were in; the diocese had approved the plan and its cost. Now he needs to raise the money to finance it.

Fr. Dave had always disliked preaching about money. He knew of a pastor in the diocese whose parishioners called "Fr. Grab-a-Dollar" because he spoke so often of the parish's need for financial support from the parishioners. Even when the weekend readings offered him the opportunity to preach on the role of money and possessions in parishioners' lives, Fr. Dave had always tried to find another theme. But now he couldn't avoid it. As pastor, it was his job to lead the campaign. He would be required to ask parishioners to commit to contributing a fixed sum of money over a number of years, over and above their regular contributions to the parish. He would not relish this task.

In reflecting on his reluctance to preach on money in general, and to lead the capital campaign in particular, he recognized three obstacles at the root of his dread of this responsibility:

- Dealing with money had never been his strong suit. He had sought ordination because of his desire to minister to others, not because he wanted to put the squeeze on them for more funding.

- He had no background in fundraising, either from his seminary training or his previous assignment.

- Weighing most on his mind was the feeling that as a fundraiser, he lacked credibility. He lived a celibate lifestyle. He had no concerns about saving to buy a home or to put his children through college. He had a lifetime job, with no worries about a layoff. How could he credibly ask his parishioners to dig deeper in their pockets than they already had?[1]

Looking for some support, Fr. Dave called a priest friend who had been a few years ahead of him in seminary and who had recently initiated a capital campaign in the parish where he was pastor. After listening to Fr. Dave, his friend calmed him down by offering two pieces of advice. First, he wouldn't have to do this alone. The diocese would recommend an experienced fundraising consultant that he could hire to guide him along the way. Second, he should immediately read a short monograph, *The Spirituality of Fundraising*, by the renowned spiritual writer Henri Nouwen that would change his whole perspective on fundraising.[2]

The Spirituality of Fundraising

In his monograph, Nouwen emphasizes that fundraising is primarily a form of ministry. It is a way of announcing the parish's vision and inviting others to join in the vision. At the same time, it is a call to conversion. The parish is offering parishioners the opportunity to discover a new way of relating to their resources. Nouwen makes the point that, as a form of ministry, fundraising is just as spiritual as visiting the sick, preaching, counseling, or the myriad of other activities that make Fr. Dave feel fulfilled.

In fact, Nouwen writes, when a pastor prayerfully commits to placing his whole trust in God, when he recognizes that he is not raising funds for himself but rather to help God build the kingdom, and if he believes that the project for which he is raising funds offers great value to donors, he will have no trouble asking for money. He is merely providing parishioners with an opportunity.

Beyond the financial impact, fundraising also calls parishioners into a new spiritual communion with the parish. It is an occasion for the pastor to convey to his parishioners his desire for the parish to get to know them better, build the community with them, and generate a lasting partnership. He is asking them for an investment in the future of the parish.

Fr. Dave can avoid the fear of being viewed as begging for money, Nouwen counsels, if his approach to perspective donors is founded on prayer and gratitude. Through prayer, pastors should experience a reorientation of their feelings about themselves and others. Gratitude flows from the recognition that who they are, and what they have, are gifts to be received and shared.

Nouwen argues that, if done properly, a person's vocation will be deepened and strengthened by fundraising.

---

1. Daniel Conway, *The Reluctant Steward Revisited: Preparing Pastors for Administrative and Financial Duties* (St. Meinrad, IN: St. Meinrad Seminary, 2002).

2. Henri J. M. Nouwen, *The Spirituality of Fundraising*, Henri Nouwen Society, 2004, http://henrinouwen.org/resources/books/bibliography/.

Reading Nouwen changed Fr. Dave's whole perspective on fundraising. It is not a chore to be avoided, it is an opportunity for growth in faith, for both his parishioners and himself!

The Essentials of Fundraising

Shortly after completing Nouwen's monograph, Fr. Dave met with Bill, the consultant recommended by the diocese. Fr. Dave immediately felt at ease with Bill. The first thing that Bill told him was that fundraising is about building relationships. People give to people. Parishioners contribute to the parish, both on a regular basis and for special projects, because they feel a relationship with other parishioners. One of Fr. Dave's responsibilities would be to develop that relationship further.

Bill emphasized repeatedly that a correctly executed capital campaign should be a faith-defining moment in the life of the parish. In addition to meeting its financial goal, it should raise (and answer) questions such as "Who are we?" "What are we about?" and "What is our purpose?"

Bill reinforced Nouwen's spirituality of fundraising message when he told Fr. Dave that throughout the process, he should focus on the "three *I*'s of fundraising": Inform, Involve, and Invest.

First, Fr. Dave needs to *inform* the parishioners by providing details of the project (in this case, the renovations to the parish hall) and how it fits both the mission and vision of the parish. Next, he needs to *invite* them to be more fully involved in all aspects of parish life, so they can view firsthand the benefits that the parish will receive from the project. Once he has accomplished these, parishioners should feel comfortable in *investing* in the parish's future by donating to the campaign.

Bill introduced Fr. Dave to one of the basic principles of fundraising, the **20-80 Rule** (sometimes referred to as the 10-90 Rule): 20 percent (or 10 percent) of the donors will contribute 80 percent (or 90 percent) of the money. That is, focus your major effort on those who are likely to make larger donations.

The ability to attract large donations requires a game plan. First, identify those prospective donors who might be in a position of making a large contribution. This could be based on factors such as the amount they contribute to the weekend collection, their reputation for being generous to other causes, or other information. It is important that someone, typically the pastor, meet with them personally. There is no substitute for a face-to-face meeting that provides the prospective donor with firsthand understanding of the campaign's goals and vision, and the pastor's ability to articulate them.

In addition to the 20-80 Rule, Bill stressed that another rule of fundraising is the **3-1 Rule**: identify three prospective donors for every gift that the campaign hopes to receive.

Fr. Dave was comforted when Bill emphasized that he did not have to contact the prospective donors alone. He should recruit a group of volunteers who will serve as the campaign planning committee. They not only make contributions themselves, but would be willing to enlist fellow parishioners to solicit on behalf of the campaign. In fact, one of the keys to a successful fundraising campaign is to have the right person approach each potential donor. It is very likely that some of the campaign's volunteers have close relationships with some fellow parishioners and would be more effective in approaching them than if Fr. Dave approached them himself.

The Fundraising Process Step by Step
Campaign Planning Committee

First, establish a **campaign planning committee**, a group of parish volunteers who will work with the pastor and the consultant. The committee should be led by cochairs to share the burden. All of the committee's members, but especially the co-chairs, must be influential parishioners with excellent reputations for supporting the parish. The committee will play a number of crucial roles in the campaign, including the recruitment of volunteers who will visit parishioners and solicit pledges for the campaign.

A capital campaign will not be successful if it is impersonal—done through direct mail or worse, the collection basket. It is a people-intensive undertaking requiring a large number of volunteers. While the pastor's leadership is essential, it is not enough. The active involvement of a motivated group of volunteers is essential to the campaign's success.

The committee works with the pastor and consultant to

- Develop a case statement
- Identify parishioners to be interviewed for the campaign feasibility study
- Generate a gift range table
- Identify a prospect list
- Establish procedures for soliciting gifts, reporting gifts, and campaign accounting
- Recruit volunteers who will meet personally with parishioners to solicit their participation in the campaign
- Monitor the progress of the campaign

Subcommittees can be established for responsibilities such as public relations or special events. The special events subcommittee would be in charge of planning events such as a parish-wide campaign kickoff event or recognition dinners for those contributing leadership gifts.

Figure 11-1
Fundraising campaign step by step

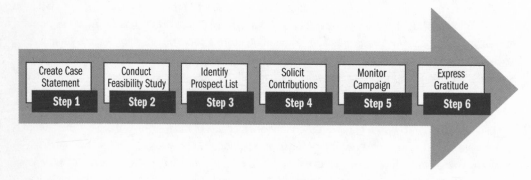

Step 1. Create Case Statement

The first task undertaken by the campaign planning committee will be to work with the pastor and the consultant in developing a **case statement**. A case statement gives the rationale for supporting the project, the motivation for contributing to the campaign. It explains the importance, relevance, and urgency of the project. It describes the project in straightforward and forceful terms. Anyone reading it should be convinced that the project is both valuable and feasible.

The case statement should include the following:

- A brief description of the parish's history, mission, and vision, placing the project in the overall context of the impact that the parish has in the lives of its parishioners and the community

- A concise description of the project: How large will it be? Is it new construction or a renovation? Where will it be located? What is the total cost? What is the capital campaign's goal?

- A justification for why the project, and the services that it will provide, are needed. How do you know?

- An explanation of how the completed project will further the parish's mission

- A specific description of the benefits, including nonfinancial benefits, that the project will provide to the parish. In other words, why does this project deserve your support?

The case statement should be the centerpiece of all communication materials (brochures, letters, etc.). It should focus on making one convincing point. Everything else in the case statement is there to support that point. It should be written so that parishioners can personally commit to the project and be able to envision the difference that project will make to parish life. There is a direct relationship between the enthusiasm for the project that the case statement displays and the enthusiasm that potential donors (parishioners) will feel for the campaign.

Step 2. Conduct Feasibility Study

Once the case statement has been finalized, the campaign planning committee works with the pastor and the consultant in identifying parishioners to be contacted while the parish performs a **feasibility study**. This is a series of confidential interviews the consultant will conduct with leading parishioners that will provide an indication of their support for the campaign, and thus the campaign's likelihood for success. It's important that someone external to the parish, such as the consultant, conduct the feasibility study in order to get a neutral assessment. Recall the 20-80 Rule. If those parishioners who are potential members of the 20 percent are not supportive, the campaign has little chance for success.

Based on the findings of the feasibility study, the consultant will advise the pastor as to the likelihood of the success of the campaign.

Step 3. Identify Prospect List and Gift Range Chart

Not everyone in the parish can be expected to contribute at the same level. Parishioners will vary in their willingness and ability to support the campaign. Another role of the campaign planning committee is to develop a **prospect list** that categorizes parishioners according to their likelihood of making a donation at a certain level.

In developing their list, the committee needs to bear in mind the 3-1 Rule: for every gift that the parish hopes to secure, they need three prospects. Table 1 demonstrates a sample **gift range chart** (without parishioner names) for a $1 million campaign.

This tool will calculate the number and size of gifts needed to achieve the fundraising goal so that resources can be adjusted appropriately.

Table 11-1
Sample gift range chart
$1 million campaign

Range	Number of Gifts Required	Number of Prospects Required	Total	Cumulative	Cumulative Percentage
100,000	1	3	100,000	100,000	10%
75,000	1	3	75,000	175,000	18%
50,000	3	6	150,000	325,000	33%
25,000	5	15	125,000	450,000	45%
20,000	5	15	100,000	550,000	55%
10,000	10	30	100,000	650,000	65%
5,000	30	90	150,000	800,000	80%
2,500	40	120	100,000	900,000	90%
1,000	50	150	50,000	950,000	95%
500	50	150	25,000	975,000	98%
LT 500	80	240	25,000	1,000,000	100%

Note that the sample gift range chart follows both the 3-1 Rule and the 20-80 Rule. There are three prospects for each gift, and 20 percent of the donors have contributed 80 percent of the total amount raised.

Donations received by those contributing at the highest level are known as **leadership gifts**. Again, recalling the 20–80 Rule, it is imperative for the success of the campaign that a handful of large gifts are received. A campaign will not succeed if it relies on many small or medium-sized donations. Once the gift range chart is established, the campaign planning committee should immediately identify the parishioners who have the inclination and the ability to contribute at the highest levels—in other words, those who are in a position to make leadership gifts.

Unless there is a compelling reason, the pastor should contact the leadership gift prospects, either by himself or accompanied by one of the cochairs of the campaign planning committee. If another member of the committee has a particularly strong relationship with a major gift prospect, that person should accompany the pastor.

The key factors in identifying those to be approached for leadership gifts include a record of generosity to the parish, a record of involvement in parish ministries, especially in leadership roles, and of course the financial wherewithal to make a large contribution. If possible, the commitment to making these gifts should be secured before the campaign is officially launched. This is often referred to as the **quiet phase** of the campaign. Ideally, the quiet phase should result in commitments amounting to 40–50 percent of the campaign goal. Announcing the leadership gifts at the time that the campaign officially kicks off is a great way to build momentum.

Step 4. Solicit Contributions

Once the campaign has been launched, the volunteer solicitors that have been recruited by the campaign planning committee begin visiting prospects. Usually, each volunteer commits to visiting five to ten prospects. But first, the volunteers must make their own gifts. They need to support the campaign before they can ask for anyone else's support.

There is a well-known fundraising saying: "You don't get 100 percent of the money that you don't ask for." No one likes to ask for money. But the volunteers should follow Henri Nouwen's recommendations.

If they approach this task through a combination of prayer and gratitude, if they recognize that they are not asking for money for themselves but to help build God's kingdom, and if they believe that the project has value, any trepidation should dissolve.

While the parish will be grateful for gifts of all sizes, large campaigns such as the one being carried out by St. Michael's can't expect to raise the money all at once. Instead, they will give donors the option of making a **pledge**, a commitment to contribute a given amount over a specified period of time, typically three to five years depending on the amount that the campaign hopes to raise. The donor spreads the gift over that period by contributing the same amount each month or quarter, depending on how the pledge is set up, until the full amount of the pledge has been contributed.

While pledging is convenient for the donor, the parish hopes that many donors (especially those making major gifts) will complete their donation as soon as possible. That is because most dioceses require that 100 percent of the cost of the capital project must be pledged, and at least 50 percent of the total amount collected, before the project can begin. The more donors who make their gift up front, the sooner the project can begin.

In addition to one-time gifts or pledges, there are other innovative ways that donors can contribute to the campaign.

Matching Gifts

Some employers will match gifts made by their employees, thus doubling the impact of the gift. The parish should distribute forms to facilitate this.

In-Kind Gifts

Depending on the relationship with the parish's building contractor, there might be opportunities for in-kind gifts that contribute toward the completion of the project. These include materials, equipment, fixtures, and furnishings. Parishioners who own their own businesses might find this alternative attractive.

Planned Giving

Planned giving involves contributions from a parishioner's estate. Typically, this allows donors to make larger gifts than they could out of their current income. In addition to benefitting the parish, there can be significant tax advantages for both the donor and the donor's beneficiaries. A planned gift could include stocks, real estate, art, life insurance, or other assets attached to the donor's estate. Parishioners who are considering making a planned giving gift should consult their tax attorney.

Online Giving

Most parishes have relationships with one or more local banks to facilitate online giving for the weekend collection. In most cases, these can be extended to the capital campaign. The advantages are the same as they are for regular support: the funds are transferred at the beginning of the month, before the parishioner's checkbook is depleted, and the burden of record keeping is eased.

Naming Opportunities

Some parishioners will be attracted by the opportunity to commemorate a loved one by attaching that person's name to part of the project. Naming opportunities can be made available for large gifts ("The John and Joan Doe Room") or for smaller gifts, such as bricks in a walkway. Another alternative is for the parish to post recognition plaques in a public place acknowledging gifts of a certain level.

Providing On-Ramps

A multiyear capital project need not rely solely on initial contributions or pledges. Over the course of a campaign, new parishioners will join the parish. They should be given the opportunity to contribute to the plan as well. In addition, parishioners' attitudes and socioeconomic status change. Some parishioners may have contributed or pledged little or nothing because of a negative attitude toward the parish or the project that has since been resolved. Others may find that their financial ability to contribute has improved since the initiation of the campaign, and they are now in a position to contribute more. These parishioners and others should be given the opportunity to join the campaign. Semiannual or annual "on-ramps" should be included in the campaign plan to enable those who would like to join the campaign or increase their contribution or pledge. These could take many forms, ranging from formal commitment weekends to seminars on the benefits of estate planning with the opportunity to use that information to rethink one's pledge. These should be low-key but firm in their appeal, following Nouwen's guidelines.

Monitoring and Record Keeping

Before the campaign has begun, there should be a system in place for tracking and documenting pledges. Most parish management software supports this function. Assign a staff person to this task. Based on the information collected, each donor should receive regular mailings from the parish detailing the progress of both the campaign and their pledge and thanking them for their support.

Over the course of the campaign, some donors will be unwilling or unable to complete their pledge. A capital campaign that collects 90 percent of its pledges is doing very well. This should be factored in when the campaign goal is first established.

Donors who fall behind on their pledge commitment should be contacted in person. Usually, there is a very good reason why the donor has fallen behind and frequently alternative arrangements can be made. In some cases, such as financial hardship, this might require a pastoral response. Under no circumstances should donors be threatened with any repercussions if they choose to not fulfill their pledge.

This process should be overseen by the campaign planning committee.

Express Gratitude

A typical parish capital campaign should run from two to four months, starting with the official kickoff and ending with a closing celebration. Of course, this will vary depending on the amount to be raised and individual parish circumstances. And, of course, pledges will continue to be paid long after the official campaign has ended. The period should be established up front so that everyone understands the parameters of the campaign.

Every gift should be followed by a thank-you note at the time the gift is made, both to express gratitude and to confirm receipt of the gift. The acknowledgment letter will also serve as a receipt for tax purposes. According to Internal Revenue Service regulations, taxpayers who claim charitable contributions are required to obtain and keep a written acknowledgment for the contribution.[3]

At the campaign's conclusion, it is important to personally thank everyone associated with the campaign, ranging from the members of the campaign planning committee to the person donating the least amount. Ways to express gratitude can include a simple personal note from the pastor to a closing celebratory dinner where the pastor moves around the room expressing his gratitude, or a closing Mass. Everyone should feel good about their participation.

---

3. For more information, see Internal Revenue Service guidelines at http://www.irs.gov/Charities-&-Non-Profits/Substantiating-Charitable-Contributions.

Stewardship

A capital campaign is an excellent time to initiate or reinforce the concept of stewardship in the parish. This is a chance to have parishioners reflect on the role of money and possessions in their lives, to consider returning to God in thanksgiving a portion of the blessings that God has bestowed on them. It is not an obligation; it is an opportunity to experience the joy of giving back to God. With the proper emphasis, enthusiasm for contributing time, talent, and treasure should persist long after the campaign has been completed. A successful capital campaign should not only raise funds, but also build community, increase participation, and leave the parish a more spiritual place than before the campaign. The capital campaign should not be conceived as an end in itself. Rather it is a means to an end: spiritual growth for parishioners.

In fact, if done well, a campaign that emphasizes a stewardship approach might find that parishioners will continue to contribute to the parish at a higher level by converting some of their pledge amount to regular weekly contributions once the campaign has ended. The spirit of generosity and the change of mind and heart that stewardship can instill in parishioners should continue well after they have completed their pledge commitment.

As a faith-based organization, the parish will likely want to institute a campaign prayer to be recited at every opportunity during the campaign. The campaign prayer is an excellent way to reinforce the stewardship component of the campaign.

The extent to which a potential consultant emphasizes a stewardship approach is one defining characteristic that will help the parish determine which consultant is right for them.

Campaign Costs

When planning for the campaign, you must factor in the costs of running the campaign. These include paying for the consultant and staff, entertainment for cultivating donors, office expenses such as supplies and postage, and campaign materials such as brochures and letters. These costs typically run 10–15 percent of the campaign goal, depending on the amount to be raised.

Chapter Summary

Fr. Dave is feeling much more relaxed about his role in the capital campaign and its chances for success. One million dollars is a lot of money to raise, and St. Michael's is far from being the wealthiest parish in the diocese. But with the guidance of consultant Bill and a dedicated and enthusiastic campaign planning committee, the project no longer seems so daunting. Fr. Dave has been in the parish long enough to make him confident that his parishioners will rally behind the campaign.

The key is to approach the project one task at a time: first, the case statement; then, the feasibility study; then, the prospect list, and so on. When broken down into specific, straightforward tasks, the whole campaign fits together nicely.

Fr. Dave is also greatly comforted by his reading of Henri Nouwen's *The Spirituality of Fundraising*. Yes, raising money, not for yourself, but for a project in which you really believe, will assist in building God's kingdom; it is truly a spiritual activity. It is rightfully a part of his ministry, even though he has been given no background in fundraising.

Once the funding for the renovations to the parish hall has been raised, the next issue is the actual construction. But Fr. Dave is confident that, with the guidance of the construction contractor and some knowledgeable parishioners, he won't need to face that alone either. After all, can that possibly be more difficult than asking people for money?

References

Conway, Daniel. *The Reluctant Steward Revisited: Preparing Pastors for Administrative and Financial Duties* (St. Meinrad, IN: St. Meinrad Seminary, 2002).

Nouwen, Henri J. M. *The Spirituality of Fundraising.* Henri Nouwen Society, 2004, henrinouwen.org/resources/books/bibliography/.

Chapter 12

Take the Next Step

O ur hypothetical Fr. Dave has completed his first budget cycle. He has implemented the internal financial controls recommended by the diocesan internal audit. He has submitted the necessary financial reports to the diocese. The capital campaign has begun. He and his team have been looking into using tools like cost/benefit analysis and breakeven analysis to enhance their decision-making processes. It has been quite a year.

What has Fr. Dave (and, we hope, you) learned from all of this activity? In addition to the specific parish financial management techniques introduced, what are the primary takeaways?

1. First, don't be intimidated. One of the primary obstacles when someone is first given responsibility for parish financial management is the unfamiliar terminology. As we've tried to demonstrate in each chapter, some of the terminology surrounding parish finances might be foreign but each concept has a specific meaning. If leaders are clear about terminology and everyone on the team is speaking the same financial language, it can bring clarity to all components of the parish financial management process.

2. Likewise, each parish financial management topic can be simplified by breaking it down into its component parts. For example, budgeting has three primary phases: formulating the budget, executing the budget, and controlling the budget. In turn, each of these phases has specific steps that when followed sequentially result in a logical progression through that phase. The same is true for implementing internal financial controls, generating financial reports, and so forth. Follow the steps mapped out in this book and a seemingly insurmountable and somewhat alien task no longer seems that intimidating.

3. Financial transparency and accountability are important. So is collaboration. We have emphasized throughout the book the importance of getting everyone involved and on board. This not only shares the workload, but also empowers staff and encourages buy-in. For example, when a staff member like the director of religious education (DRE) has input into formulating the budget and understands the constraints inherent in that process, that same DRE will be more likely to understand the issues and be more accepting when it comes to budget control.

4. In many cases, parish financial management is as much an art as a science. Much of it involves forecasting and estimating. Don't discount the experience of the parish staff when making parish financial management decisions. Likewise, once the pastor and his team have been through the budget process, prepared financial reports, or implemented internal financial controls, they will be prepared in the future to nuance the strict scientific approach to meet the needs of their particular parish's situation.

5. Chancery officials are your friends—even the auditor. Don't be afraid to rely on them if you run into trouble. They are there not only to help you resolve parish financial management issues but also to prevent problems before they happen.

6. Sometimes parish financial management involves making decisions that offend staff or parishioners, as in the case of implementing internal financial controls. The parish leadership's response? "This is for your own protection." It is also for the pastor's protection.

7. Parish financial management is not about money. It about the parish's mission, vision, and goals, and using the resources at the parish's disposal to achieve them. It is about connecting parish priorities with its resources. It is about planning and making effective decisions on behalf of parishioners. When viewed in this light, it is clear that it is part of ministry. The pastor and staff need to recognize that formulating, executing, and controlling the budget are important components of their ministry to the parish. So is the implementation of internal financial controls and the other topics covered in this book. If nothing else, sound parish financial management is required of the pastor and staff as part of stewardship.

8. This leads into the importance that faith must play in the financial management of a faith-based organization like a parish. All of the principles, methods, tools, and tips in this book are centered on faith. Prayer and discernment are critical components of the process in every parish financial decision.

While this book has been written specifically for those involved in the financial management of a parish, it should be clear that the methodology presented is applicable to any faith-based organization. It is also scalable. Large, small, and medium-sized parishes and other faith-based organizations can apply the concepts at whatever level of detail makes the most sense in their situation. The point is to address the primary components. For example, in the budget process, each parish needs to go through the three phases of formulating, executing, and controlling. The amount of detail in each step might differ by size and complexity, but each of these phases must be addressed nonetheless.

What is the next step? At some point, the parish's pastoral plan needs review. The parish budget is a reflection of the parish's pastoral plan. Pastoral plans have a three- to five-year shelf life and are typically reviewed during that period to ensure that the goals, objectives, and strategies in the plan are still relevant. The parish budget needs to be in constant coordination with the parish priorities as stated in the pastoral plan. Any revision in the plan should automatically be reflected in the next parish budget.

Now you are prepared to dive into the previously mystifying worlds of parish budgeting, financial reporting, internal financial controls, and financial decision making and fundraising. You have all of the tools that you need to be successful at each. Compared with some of the other challenges that parishes and their leaders face, parish financial management should now be among the least of your concerns!

Glossary

Accounting—Accounting is the systematic means of recording, managing, reporting, and communicating financial actions of an organization (chap. 9).

Accounting Equation—Assets equal liabilities plus net assets, the foundation for double-entry accounting (chap. 9).

Accrual Basis—An accounting system that records income when earned rather than when cash is received, and expenses when incurred rather than when a bill is paid (chap. 9).

Activity-Based Resourcing (ABR)—Analysis to determine the amount of resources (money, time, people) necessary to undertake or complete an activity such as a program, project, specific task, or service (chap. 10).

Apportionment—A structured budget execution procedure to release funds at specific periods throughout the fiscal year (e.g., July 1, October 1, January 1, April 1). This process provides clear guidelines on how much money is available for a specific program or spending line item for a given period (chap. 6).

Assets—Resources that have value. Parish assets may include cash available from the parish checking and savings accounts, receivables such as pledges, items owned by the parish such as computer equipment, and other fixed assets like the parish buildings (chap. 9).

Assumptions, Budget—Documentation of expectations that affect financial plans. May include data used for projecting income and expense projections and outlines factors that influence the budget plan (chap. 2).

Authority, Budget—Funding ceiling over which a program or category of spending cannot pass for a given period (chap. 6).

Balanced Budget—Achieved when income minus expenses are equal or greater than zero (chap. 5).

Benefit/Cost Analysis (BCA)—A systematic approach that compares and contrasts the qualitative and quantitative benefits and costs associated with alternative options. Similar terms associated with this technique are cost/benefit analysis and alternatives analysis (chap. 10).

Benefit/Cost Ratio (BCR)—Calculation to compare the benefits to the costs for alternative options. Used as a component of benefit/costs analysis (chap. 10).

Bottom-Up Budgeting—Budget method, also referred to as zero-based budgeting, whereby resources are built from the lowest income/expense elements and then rolled up into the total budget request. From zero, each cost element is developed and justified (chap. 4).

Breakeven Analysis—Evaluation technique to determine at what point a program, project, or event will pay for itself (chap. 10).

Budget—Planning and management tool for executing priorities by projecting, allocating, and managing the money you receive and the money you plan to spend (chap. 1).

Budget Category Impact Percentage (BCIP)—Calculation to assess the relative size of a specific budget category as compared to the total spending for the overall income or expense category. It is a helpful analysis technique used during financial planning and analysis (chap. 5).

Budget Formulation Calendar—Schedule of budget activities that includes major milestones and deadlines for budget development (chap. 3).

Budget Guidance Document—Guidelines distributed at the start of the budget formulation phase that outline current assumptions and expectations, as the budget is prepared (chap. 3).

Budget Lifecycle—Roadmap to help guide parish budget process that includes three phases that build upon one another: budget formulation, execution, and control (chap. 1).

Buy-In, Budget—Ownership and understanding of preliminary budget among stakeholders (e.g., staff, parishioners, finance and pastoral councils) before final budget approval (chap. 1).

Campaign Planning Committee—A group of parish volunteers who work with the pastor and the consultant. It plays a number of crucial roles in a capital campaign, including the recruitment of volunteers who will visit parishioners and solicit pledges for the campaign (chap. 11).

Capital Assets—Assets (items that have value) with useful lives extending beyond the year in which they are purchased or put into service. Examples include parish facilities, equipment, and technology (chap. 2).

Capital Budget—Resourcing plan for updating, repairing, maintaining, or purchasing assets whose value extends beyond a one-year window (chap. 2).

Capital Campaign—A concentrated fundraising effort intended to raise a specific sum of money within a defined time period to meet the varied needs of an organization (chap. 11).

Case Statement—The rationale for supporting a capital project, explaining the importance, relevance, and urgency of the project (chap. 11).

Cash Basis—An accounting system under which revenues are recorded when cash is received and expenses are recorded when cash is paid out (chap. 9).

Cash Flow Budget—Financial plan that displays anticipated actual income/receipts and expenditures for a given period. Unlike a linear budget that spreads income and expenses evenly over a period, the cash flow budget presents a realistic month-to-month (or week or day) projection of cash received and cash to be expended (chap. 5).

Categories, Budget—Classifications for the money that is received, money spent, and money saved. Examples include Sunday collections, personnel expenses, supplies, and equipment (chap. 2).

Chart of Accounts (COA)—Hierarchical in format, a COA is a coding system for the variety of account types, programs, and the variety of income and spending categories. A series of digits make up the structure for understanding the type, level, and detailed information related to an account or budget line item (chap. 9).

Check Requests—Standard procedure at parishes for the purposes of issuing checks for advances, commitments (obligations), or reimbursements (chap. 6).

Code of Canon Law—Code of ecclesiastical laws governing the Catholic Church (chap. 9).

Cost Avoidance—The value received from the difference between what we actually spend and what we would spend if we determine a course of action. To determine value, answer the question, "How much will the parish *save in the future*?" (chap. 9)

Cost Element—Category of cost (or type of cost) (chap. 4).

Costs Savings—Refers to money now available that was previously unavailable because it was budgeted or allocated for a given expense. To determine value, answer the question, "How much *less* will the parish need to spend on a given category that has been previously budgeted/spent?" (chap. 10).

Credit—Bookkeeping term that either increases an asset or expense account, or decreases a liability or net asset account (chap. 9).

Debit—Bookkeeping term that either increases a liability or net asset, or decreases an asset or expense account (chap. 9).

Deficit—Excess of expenses over income (chap. 5).

Defined Benefit Plan—Employer-offered retirement plan, commonly known as a pension plan, whereby the employer guarantees the employee a certain benefit under certain conditions (chap. 5).

Defined Contribution Plan—Employer-offered retirement plan whereby the employer contributes a set percentage of the employee's salary to an independent investment pool. The employee also has the opportunity to contribute to a plan pretax (up to certain limits) (chap. 5).

Direct Costs/Resources—Resources (money, time, people) that have a direct relationship to a service or program (chap. 10).

Discounting—The reverse of compound interest; a process in which interest that could be earned over time is deducted from a future payment to determine how much the future payment is worth at the present time (chap. 10).

Double-Entry Accounting—Standard accounting procedure whereby every financial transaction is recorded as a debit or credit in ledgers and journals to ensure that both sides of the accounting equation are in balance (chap. 9).

Execution, Budget—Phase of budget lifecycle that begins after the budget is approved. Common strategies during this phase include apportioning money to help manage cash flow, creating clear and understandable parish expense requisition processes, and developing efficient payment and processing procedures for effective resource management (chap. 1).

External Audit—A periodic or impromptu review conducted by independent certified accountants to determine if the organization's accounting records are accurate and complete, prepared in accordance with the requirements of GAAP, and that the statements prepared from the accounts fairly present the organization's financial position, and the results of its financial operations (chap. 8).

Feasibility Study—A series of confidential interviews conducted by a campaign consultant with leading parishioners that provides an indication of the support for the campaign, and thus the campaign's likelihood for success (chap. 11).

Financial Accounting Standards Board (FASB)—The governing board that regulates the wide variety of rules and regulations for accounting in the United States (chap. 8).

Financial Management—Planning, organizing, directing, and controlling the financial activities of the organization. Focuses on generating financial information that can be used to improve decisions (chap. 9).

Financial Statements—Financial reports that provide information about the parish's financial position and the results of activities. Key financial statements include the statements of financial position, activities, and cash flows (chap. 9).

Fiscal Year (FY)—Period of time for which an organization plans the use of funds and reports financial status (chap. 2).

Fixed Costs—Expenses that do not change as volume increases or decreases for services offered (chap. 5).

Forecasting—Method of predicting, projecting, and calculating information based on the study and analysis of available pertinent data (chap. 5).

Formulation, Budget—Budget lifecycle phase that includes preparation, documentation of assumptions, and projecting income, expenses, and other resources (chap. 1).

Generally Accepted Accounting Principles (GAAP)—The set of rules that must be followed for the organization's financial statements to be deemed a fair presentation of the organization's financial position and results of operations (chap. 9).

Gift Range Chart—Tool that calculates the number and size of gifts needed to achieve a capital campaign's fundraising goal (chap. 11).

Incremental Budgeting—Budget method whereby a specific amount or percentage increase or decrease is applied across budget categories to create a budget proposal (chap. 4).

Indirect Resources—Resources (money, time, people) that are not directly related to a specific activity or program but provide general support to an activity (chap. 10).

Internal Audit—A means for improving an organization's governance, risk management, and management controls by providing recognition and recommendations based on analyses and appraisals of data and business processes (chap. 8).

Internal Financial Controls—A process for assuring achievement of an organization's objectives in operational effectiveness and efficiency, reliable financial reporting, and compliance with laws, regulations, and policies (chap. 8).

Invoices—Standard document requested by vendors or contractors for payment (chap. 6).

Leadership Gifts—Donations received by those contributing at the highest level (chap. 11).

Liabilities—Financial obligations for what the parish owes to others (chap. 9).

Lifecycle Costs—Cost elements for a particular investment that includes direct and indirect initial costs, plus any periodic or continuing costs of operation and maintenance (chap. 10).

Liquidity—Financial concept for how quickly an asset can be turned into cash (chap. 9)

Management Letter—A management letter communicates deficiencies and weaknesses in a company's organizational structure that might result in the inaccurate collection of data for financial reporting or the risk of theft (chap. 8).

Master Budget—Comprehensive financial plan that includes operating and capital budgets and parish accounts and investments (chap. 2).

Matching Gifts—Some employers will match gifts made by their employees to a capital campaign, thus doubling the impact of the gift (chap. 11).

Material Weaknesses—Deficiencies in internal controls that present the prospect that the organization's financial statements may contain misstatements that can't be detected or prevented (chap. 8).

Modified Cash Basis—Accounting system that uses a cash basis to record income as it is deposited and expenses when they are paid; however, when financial reports are pulled for a given period, they also include outstanding accounts receivable and/or accounts payable (chap. 9).

Net Assets—Classified as unrestricted net assets, temporarily restricted net assets, or permanently restricted net assets (chap. 9).

Net # Days—Standard payment term that means that the purchaser of goods must pay the seller on or before # (number) of calendar days from which the goods or services were obtained (chap. 6).

"On-Ramp"—The opportunity for new parishioners to contribute to a capital campaign while the campaign is in its midst (chap. 11).

Operating Budget—Plan for addressing the day-to-day income and expenses of managing the parish. This is the plan for projecting how much money is expected into the parish (income) and how much money will be spent (expenses) (chap. 2).

Operating Expense—Categories of spending to maintain everyday costs of keeping the parish running smoothly (chap. 2).

Operating Income—Available resources for the day-to-day functioning of the parish (chap. 2).

Parish Requisition Form—Standard template for the disbursement of funds (chap. 6).

Permanently Restricted Net Assets—Contributions with restrictions placed by the donor that cannot be removed by actions of the parish or the passage of time. An example of this is the donation that must be held in perpetuity, meaning that the principal donation must never be used (chap. 9).

Planned Giving—Contributions from a parishioner's estate, such as stocks, real estate, art, life insurance, or other assets attached to the donor's estate (chap. 11).

Pledge—A commitment to contribute a given amount over a specified period of time to a financial campaign (chap. 11).

Preliminary Budget—Plan consolidates income, expense, and program justification information for review before budget approval (chap. 3).

Present Value—Value of future receipts or payments discounted to the present (chap. 10).

Prospect list—Categorizes parishioners according to their likelihood of making a donation to a capital campaign at a certain level (chap. 11).

Qualitative Benefits—Benefits received that do not necessarily have monetary value but improve, enhance, or bring additional value to the parish in other ways. Examples include strategic, direct user, social, and operational benefits (chap. 10).

Qualitative Factor Scoring—Evaluation method to analyze qualitative factors as a component of benefit/cost analysis (chap. 10).

Quantitative Benefits—Benefits received that can be valued or measured in some numerical or monetary amount. Also referred to as tangible benefits; examples include cost savings and cost avoidance (chap. 10).

QUEST Analysis—Technique to analyze budget to uncover, focus, and respond to changing circumstances surrounding any type of financial plans. Process includes questioning (Q), understanding (U), evaluating (E), solving (S), and tracking (T) plans (chap. 7).

Quiet Phase—Those gifts secured before a capital campaign is officially launched (chap. 11).

Reallocation—The adjustment of resources between or within budget categories, also referred to as fund reprogramming (chap. 7).

Restricted Assets—Assets that have been made for a specific and designated purpose and must only be used for those purposes (chap. 9).

Revenues—The amounts of money the parish has received or is entitled to receive (chap. 9).

Segmentation of Duties—An approach to internal financial controls based on shared responsibilities related to the collection, deposit, disbursement, and reconciling of parish funds (chap. 8).

Sensitivity Analysis—Analyze outcomes using varying assumptions, data, and predictions. Method is often referred to as "what if analysis" (chap. 5).

Statement of Activities—Financial report that displays the current revenue, expenses, and the difference between the two as change in net assets for a given period of time (e.g., July 1–June 30). Businesses will refer to this report as "income statement" (chap. 9).

Statement of Cash Flows—Financial report that details cash flow from operations, investment, and financing activities for a given period (e.g., July 1–June 30) (chap. 9).

Statement of Financial Position—Financial report that displays assets owned, liabilities owed, and net assets at a specific point in time. Financial resources are reported in order of liquidity (e.g., June 30). Businesses will refer to this report as "the balance sheet" (chap. 9).

Surplus—Excess of income over expenses (chap. 5).

Tamper-Proof Bag—Security bags for storing collection funds and other parish revenue that feature a tamper evident closure. After inserting the contents, the security bag is sealed. If the closure is opened, it will show some form of tamper evidence (chap. 8).

Temporarily Restricted Assets—Assets that are limited by donor-imposed stipulations that either expire by the passage of time or are fulfilled by actions of the parish (chap. 9).

3–1 Rule—Three prospective donors must be identified for every gift that a capital campaign hopes to receive (chap. 11).

Time Value of Money—Principle based on the premise that a dollar today is more valuable than a dollar in the future (chap. 10).

Top-Down Budgeting—Budget method whereby resources are allocated at a high level and details are then worked out based on the amount of projected funding (chap. 4).

20–80 Rule—20 percent of the donors will contribute 80 percent of the money to a capital campaign (chap. 11).

Unrestricted Assets—Assets available for any purpose after all money is received and bills paid (chap. 9).

Variable Costs—Expenses that directly change as a result of the variation in the volume of services delivered (chap. 5).

Variance Amount—Calculation of amount difference between budgeted and actual amounts of income or expenditures (chap. 7).

Variance Analysis—Reporting tool to review, analyze, and take action based on the difference between budgeted and actual income and expenditures (chap. 7).

Variance Percentage—Calculation of percent difference between the budgeted and actual income and expenditures per category (chap. 7).

Zero-Based Budgeting—Budget method, also referred to as bottom-up budgeting, whereby resources are built from the lowest income/expense elements and then rolled up into the total budget request. From zero, each cost element is developed and justified (chap. 4).

Index